The Future of Latin American Library Collections and Research: Contributing and Adapting to New Trends in Research Libraries

SALALM Secretariat
Latin American Library
Tulane University

The Future of Latin American Library Collections and Research: Contributing and Adapting to New Trends in Research Libraries

Papers of the Fifty-Fifth Annual Meeting of the
SEMINAR ON THE ACQUISITION OF
LATIN AMERICAN LIBRARY MATERIALS

Providence, Rhode Island
July 23–27, 2010

Fernando Acosta-Rodríguez
Editor

SALALM Secretariat
Tulane University
Latin American Library
Howard-Tilton Memorial Library
New Orleans, Louisiana

ISBN: 0-917617-86-X

Copyright © 2012 by SALALM, Inc.

All rights reserved

Printed in the United States of America

Contents

Preface

For SALALM LV, I chose to depart from the usual practice of dedicating the conference to a timely academic theme in the humanities or social sciences. I sought instead to have a forum for examining recent systemic shifts in the areas of publishing, information access, and scholarly communication; the implications for the development of Latin American research library collections; and, more broadly, the implications for how research libraries will continue to document and make available the region's intellectual and creative production. Having a better understanding of these developments is, in my view, crucial for Latin American studies librarians and other information specialists because they are certain to have consequences, and perhaps not always positive ones, on the possibilities for future Latin American studies scholarship and intellectual engagement with the region. Hence, the objective of the conference was to stimulate analysis and discussion of recent trends and their many manifestations by putting together a rich and diverse array of panels, roundtables, and workshops that paid special attention to the opportunities, risks, and consequences presented by them and to the strategies which SALALM, its members, and other stake holders are—or could be—implementing in order to adapt and shape future outcomes.

The first three contributions in the volume, including the text of the tone-setting keynote address offered by Deborah Jakubs, the Rita DiGiallonardo Holloway University Librarian and Vice Provost for Library Affairs at Duke University, are representative of some of the broad picture perspectives that were presented during the conference. The others deal with concrete and often innovative experiences in the areas of collection building, documenting, archiving, cataloging, and teaching. Two of them describe experiences particular to Latin America. I hope that readers will find them as engaging and thought-provoking as I did.

These pages, however, do not include several presentations, roundtables, and meetings that, though not producing formal papers for the volume, tremendously enriched the discussions and learning that took place during the conference. Particularly relevant to the central theme were the contributions by David Block (University of Texas at Austin), Dan Hazen (Harvard), and James Simon (CRL) during the first conference panel. Also notable were the two roundtables on cooperative collection development coordinated by Lynn Shirey (Harvard); the roundtable on the evolving roles of Latin American studies librarians organized by Jesús Alonso-Regalado (University at Albany, SUNY) and Anne Barnhart (University of West Georgia); and the Pecha Kucha event organized by Alison Hicks (University of Colorado), featuring snapshots of innovative library practices. I strongly encourage readers interested in these and many other stimulating discussions that transpired during SALALM LV to review the conference program reproduced in this volume and to consult the summaries of the presentations found in the *SALALM Newsletter* issues for December 2010 and February 2011. Both can be found at http://salalm.org/publications/salalm-newsletter/.

I am immensely grateful to Patricia Figueroa, Local Arrangements Chair, and to the Brown University Library, the Center for Latin American and Caribbean Studies, and the John Carter Brown Library for making the conference not only possible but thoroughly enjoyable. I am also most grateful to the Princeton University Library for its generous sponsorship of SALALM LV; to Hortensia Calvo and Carol Avila at the SALALM Secretariat at Tulane University for their support and advice with conference preparations; to the SALALM Libreros for their participation and support; and to Orchid Mazurkiewicz, Editorial Board Chair, for her assistance and diligence in getting these papers edited and published. Finally, I want to express my sincere appreciation to our keynote speaker, Deborah Jakubs, and to all the committee chairs, panel organizers, and presenters for their help in organizing a successful meeting.

Fernando Acosta-Rodríguez

Keynote Address

1. A Library by Any Other Name: Change, Adaptation, Transformation

Deborah Jakubs

It is a great honor for me to have the opportunity to speak to you today, to return to my roots here in SALALM, where I have made many lasting friendships with library and bookdealer colleagues from whom I have learned so much over the years. Perhaps I can give a little bit back with my remarks today. I hope so.

It is wonderful to note that SALALM has been alive and well for fifty-five years. During these five-plus decades, change has been our constant companion, and one of SALALM's many strengths has been the organization's—and its members'—capacity to recognize change, regroup and adapt to it, and to incorporate change into its character and mission. The ambitious agenda for this meeting clearly demonstrates the breadth of interests and expertise among the membership and highlights the many opportunities ahead.

Today I would like to talk with you about changes and challenges I see from my current perspective as the University Librarian and Vice Provost for Library Affairs at Duke University. The title of my presentation is derived from the many times I have been asked if we "still need libraries," or if "we should change the name" to reflect more accurately what happens in libraries these days. My response is always the same: that it has nothing to do with the word "library" and everything to do with how we define that word and how the definition has changed, particularly in the past decade. The old interpretation of "library" was narrow; the new meaning is very broad, and our mission is expanding all the time. So it is time to take a fresh look at the work of libraries and discard the old image.

First, I want to share some information on trends in area studies that I have collected in preparation for two recent public presentations: the first to the Council on East Asian Libraries (CEAL) at the meeting of the Asian Studies Association, as part of a panel on "The Future of Foreign Language Collections in Transformational Times: What is at Stake?" and, second, to the Association of Research Libraries (ARL) membership in a session on "Recalibrating Research Libraries' Approaches to Global Collections and Expertise." In both cases, I was reporting on and interpreting dynamics that come to bear on area studies librarianship and global resources. I hope that the conclusions I drew from my preparation for those presentations, and from the comments they elicited, will be of interest. I will also offer some advice and raise some questions that might inform a conversation among us later.

I will discuss some general trends. WorldCat may be an imperfect tool, but an analysis of its contents can give some indication as to trends in collecting area studies materials among the member libraries. In the two previous talks I mentioned, entitled "Are Our Worries Over? Signs of Hope for International Collections and Services," and "Are We There Yet? Trends in Global Collections and Services," I provided an update on the state of area studies collecting, particularly following the establishment of the Global Resources Program at ARL, now the Global Resources Network hosted by the Center for Research Libraries (CRL). The conclusions I drew in those presentations have relevance for SALALM and for today's discussion, so I will share some of them with you today.

As I told the CEAL audience, for some time the area studies library community has worried that area studies materials are under-collected by research libraries and used by relatively few researchers, and thus even further threatened as budgets tighten, measures of use (potential or actual) negatively influence collection development decisions, and libraries make an inevitable transition to ever-increasing reliance on digital resources. Furthermore, there is concern that the specialists who identify, acquire, process, and create access to such materials are in short supply, and the pipeline is very narrow. Fears that future scholars who want to use non-English resources will find only sparse collections have added urgency to our mission to address this situation. As a result of these concerns, and thanks to the efforts of many individuals, numerous cooperative projects have been created and have borne fruit in many cases. We know much more now than we ever have about the nature of our collections. We have employed technology to build robust new means of access, and we are doing a much better job of sharing the materials we have. However, there is still a nagging sense that we are falling behind, that area studies collections will be lost in the transformation to a digital world.

Now we have new worries about the rising costs of access to electronic information, and especially the impact on our ability to continue to acquire traditional (print) resources. We are concerned about the availability of full-text databases—whether they are being developed for, or in, all countries, on compatible platforms, and how they will be archived. We see faculty turning to new kinds of resources, for example, new media and visual materials, and we wonder how to acquire or license and provide ongoing access to those sources, which are proving to be increasingly important to the broad field of cultural studies and beyond. Research and teaching interests have expanded greatly, and interdisciplinary collaborations are also putting pressure on the ability of libraries to satisfy the wide-ranging needs of scholars and students, ever more quickly. New topics and new technologies: how do we keep track of it all, identify the sources, and pay for everything? Also, there is the duality of our world, in which we continue to acquire print materials and primary resources while dedicating more of our funds to licensing digital access. We worry that our parent institutions do not fully appreciate our cause, our needs, and our concerns in the larger budget struggles.

I understand the worries because I used to be a worrier. I was a major worrier about the crisis in foreign acquisitions, but it is time to put those old concerns aside and to focus on the successes we have had in expanding access to scholarly resources, capitalizing on technological means, and carving out a broader role for area studies. It is also important to ensure that area studies library operations are front and center in the new directions research libraries are taking. The future is bright and the opportunities are numerous. Here are some trends I see. Even some of those worries can work to our advantage.

From the crisis in foreign acquisitions, addressed by the Global Resources Network and its component projects, including the Latin Americanist Research Resources Project (LARRP), have come many digital projects that put area studies at the forefront of new developments that expand access for scholars to the materials they need, and which also strengthen the collaborations that have long characterized Latin American studies librarianship. This is especially important in the transition from print to digital, as we participate in the development of new models of digital dissemination. The area studies library community has provided leaders for these initiatives and has developed, and continues to develop, models that have broader applicability.

From the image of few users of exotic materials in strange languages, area studies has been transformed by interests of faculty from across the disciplines whose work involves new topics, new media, and new collaborations. Area studies specialists are the original interdisciplinarians, after all, a fact that should be emphasized at a time when so many universities are making interdisciplinarity a strategic goal of academic programs. This is an opportunity to address a different set of needs and to work closely with other subject specialists and vendors.

Universities are globalizing and encouraging cross-departmental, cross-school, and interinstitutional collaborations with an international focus, such as global health. More and more universities are establishing campuses abroad. This highlights the collections on Latin America and other regions as well as giving us opportunities to work with new and different groups of faculty and students.

The potential for increased outsourcing—of cataloging, for example—provides libraries with the opportunity to reallocate resources and deploy staff in new ways, while strengthening the relationships with book vendors who are providing new, valuable services.

Area studies collections are special collections. Foreign-language collections are integral to research libraries. It is our duty to collect broadly, to support the needs of researchers, and to consider the scholarly record internationally.

As libraries focus on expanding access to their distinctive collections via digitization projects, area studies will become more visible.

Finally, university librarians are paying attention. The theme of the ARL meeting in late April 2010 was "Globalization of Higher Education and Research Libraries" and featured presentations with a global focus on intellectual property, scholarly communication, partnerships across borders, multicountry universities, and other topics. The panel on which I participated, "Recalibrating Research Libraries' Approach to Global Resources," addressed such questions as the following: Are ARL libraries going to continue to build comprehensive collections of global publications and resources from all world areas? Is this an element that defines the research library in relation to the academic and research programs at our institutions? Are there opportunities for new forms of collaboration in the acquisition, cataloging, housing, use, and preservation of our global collections? How are we going to recruit the staff who have the subject, language, cultural, and technical skills to support global collection development? In addition, ARL has established a new task force to determine ways in which the organization can become more international. These are all good signs.

In his invitation to speak, Fernando Acosta-Rodríguez asked that I share some "big picture reflections." I believe that our new Duke University Libraries strategic plan, *Sharpening Our Vision,* can help focus those reflections. The plan is a concise framework, carefully and thoughtfully constructed, that contains/ supports the key elements of the work of research libraries today. I am sure it is similar to the strategic directions of other libraries. These dynamics are pervasive, and Latin American studies librarians will see a role for themselves in each area. I would suggest that we look for more ways to integrate our work with that of others, rather than maintaining a distance. In many ways, the organizational chart is just a bureaucratic convenience. Through cross-departmental and cross-unit engagement, libraries, like universities, avoid silos; our work within the library and within the wider university is increasingly collaborative, as it has long been within SALALM interinstitutionally and internationally. This is evident from a brief examination of Duke's strategic goals, and this look will also convey the relevance of my subtitle today: change, adaptation, transformation.

Improve the User Experience: Understand library users' research and library experiences and use that information to shape collections, spaces, and services.

Evaluating and assessing library services are increasingly important for justifying budget expenditures and for improving those services. The better we understand what users want and how they do their work, the more successful we will be in meeting those needs—and thus in demonstrating the value libraries add to the research process and student learning. Acting quickly to improve services, basing recommendations on data when possible, and encouraging innovation will all ensure that the library, its staff, and their responsiveness are recognized and appreciated.

Provide Digital Content, Tools, and Services: Offer services and scholarly resources in formats that best fit user needs.

It is a priority to increase the library's capacity to create, acquire, and manage digital scholarly content in a diverse range of formats, as well as to facilitate its discovery. Digital content in some cases is replacing print (journals, for example) and, in others, content is reformatted to be more widely accessible through digital means.

Develop New Research and Teaching Partnerships: Encourage new strategies for interacting and working with users, collaborating with other groups, and embedding staff and services at the right place in users' workflows.

Whether through e-science, e-scholarship, or e-publishing initiatives, librarians have many opportunities to partner with faculty, departments, programs, and institutes on campus to develop innovative projects and services. This is a new and welcome role. It offers a vantage point from which to understand how the library might configure or reconfigure its services, and how individual librarians and library staff might become more directly engaged with users. It also encourages cross-departmental collaborations within the library and a flexible organizational model.

Support University Priorities: Articulate how the libraries' collections, services, and initiatives align with the university priorities of excellence in research and teaching, internationalization, interdisciplinarity, and knowledge in the service of society.

As University Librarian, it is critically important to me that the library be seen as the intellectual center of the campus, and that our collections and services transparently and actively support the university's directions. The better we understand those priorities, the more we can reflect them in our work, our planning, and our external communications.

Enhance Library Spaces: Ensure that the libraries' physical spaces are developed in coordination with the evolution of the teaching and research needs of the university.

In addition to the question of whether we should change the name "library," another I am frequently—even more frequently—asked is whether we still need physical libraries. I can only speak directly for Duke, where many more people than ever are coming to the libraries and staying longer. Our extensive building and renovation project, in which we nearly doubled our space, resulted in a dramatic increase in visits and also in the number of print books being checked out, a fact that for some reason comes as a surprise to many folks. We are always watching for ways to adapt the space; for example, given the heavy emphasis on interdisciplinary work and a reliance on more e-resources in the sciences, we integrated three science branches into the main library, one each summer, over the past three years.

In conclusion, to me the big picture for libraries looks like this:

- increasing engagement for staff beyond the physical walls of the library—within the university, the region, nationally, internationally

- staying on top of new trends in scholarship, publishing, and library services, and sharing that knowledge, integrating it into our work, anticipating, identifying, and adapting to changes

- increasing focus on assessment and accountability

- encouraging and rewarding creativity, innovation, and collaboration

- increasing focus on "going where the user is"—for example, delivery to mobile devices

- not being afraid of trying new things, even if they might fail—we will learn from the experience

- viewing collections not as print and digital, but just collections, integrated means of conveying information and sharing scholarship

- reaching the point when the most innovative ideas and services become a natural part of our daily work, not perceived as add-ons to our "regular" work

- budget pressures help identify what we can stop doing in order to do new things; early retirements gave us the opportunity to consolidate functions and reallocate positions to new services

- ensuring that staff have the requisite skills and training to meet the challenges we face

- library staff will bring diverse experiences and take different paths to library work

- library as place, library as collection

Now is a good time to take a hard look at SALALM's stated mission, given the changes in scholarly communication, publishing, and libraries. According to the website, the mission *assumes* the existence of a user (of bibliographic information, publications, collections, cooperation) but does not explicitly mention a focus on the changing needs of researchers, students, and teachers and the new means by which libraries address them—all themes so evident in this meeting's agenda. Nor does the impact of the rapidly evolving role of libraries and librarians or the expanded scope of publishers and vendors appear in SALALM's mission, although the actual work of SALALM recognizes these changes.

As we celebrate SALALM at this 55th annual meeting, I encourage you to make sure that the mission adequately represents the organization's achievements and aspirations, in light of the environment in which we are living and working, and that it reflects the change, adaptation, and transformation of the new definition of "library." SALALM has much to celebrate and still more to anticipate.

Papers

2. ¿Qué sabemos del futuro del libro?: el SALALM, los libreros y el libro que está por venir

Álvaro Risso

Es muy complejo, es muy difícil poder resumir en una corta charla todo lo que actualmente sucede en el mundo del libro, y a la vez intentar proyectar lo que acontecerá en el futuro inmediato de la industria editorial, así como lo que ocurrirá con el oficio del librero y con las librerías. Entendemos que como hablaremos de los tiempos que se vienen, el panorama que expondremos contiene más intuiciones que certezas.

Los profesionales del libro contamos con mucha información sobre el tema, muchas ideas y teorías, que intentaremos resumir en esta breve presentación. Vamos a desarrollar algunos conceptos, que hemos dividido en tres partes.

1. Los demasiados libros

Para comprender mejor las transformaciones del mundo del libro, debemos empezar por reconocer los problemas y las patologías que la propia industria editorial ha provocado en los mercados, situándonos en lo que fue la advertencia, el llamado de alerta más claro de lo que iba a ocurrir: *los demasiados libros*.

Con este título, el escritor mexicano Gabriel Zaid publicó en 1996 un lúcido ensayo en el cual ponía de manifiesto las dificultades que causan la enorme cantidad de ejemplares que se publican en el planeta año tras año. Si bien la historia del libro moderno cuenta ya con 550 años, desde Gutemberg hasta hoy, los demasiados libros son un fenómeno que aparece en los últimos veinticinco años, cuando irrumpe la fabricación masiva de ediciones. Zaid pronosticó lo que vendría, y nos hizo ver, ya en 1996, que "los demasiados libros son un hecho central para entender el problema del libro, contra los diagnósticos y remedios convencionales."[1]

El ritmo de crecimiento anual en la cantidad de libros que se han publicado en este último cuarto de siglo es asombrosa, y al menos por ahora, no ha decaído. Afirma Zaid: "La humanidad publica un libro cada medio minuto… los libros se publican a tal velocidad que nos vuelven cada día más incultos. Si uno leyera un libro diario, estaría dejando de leer cuatro publicados el mismo día."[2] ¿A qué se debe y cómo se explica esta sobre abundancia de oferta y qué inconvenientes provoca? Hay varias explicaciones.

La primera tiene que ver con que los requisitos para ingresar en el comercio del libro son muy escasos, debido a que los costos se han reducido considerablemente.

Hoy en día, para poner en marcha una pequeña editorial no se necesitan grandes inversiones, a lo que se agrega que cualquier autor aficionado puede publicar su propio libro. La vanidad de muchos autores que creen que sus textos merecen ser editados, hace que la multiplicación sea incesante.

Otra razón visible se debe a la imparable sucesión de títulos que lanzan algunos editores, en la incansable búsqueda del *bestseller*. Hay grandes editoriales que destinan importantes recursos tratando de acertar con alguna obra, y conseguir el tan ansiado éxito de ventas. Pero por el camino quedarán muchos libros de escasa comercialización, poca o nula difusión y vida efímera.

Otro libro al que me quiero referir y que estudia con profundidad este fenómeno, es el de los españoles Jordi Nadal y Francisco García, titulado *Libros o velocidad*, publicado como parte de la colección *Libros sobre libros* a cargo de Fondo de Cultura Económica. Aquí hay textos y opiniones que ilustran el fenómeno de la excesiva cantidad de libros. Jordi Nadal afirma que:

> Cuando todo vale, cuando todo se puede editar, cuando todos podemos salir en televisión, cuando no hay una selección, cuando todo está disponible, estamos mayormente expuestos a la confusión….
>
> …Tener las máximas facilidades para editar gracias a las nuevas tecnologías no presupone que vayan a florecer mejores escritores. Ni que cualquiera pueda ser editor….
>
> …No todo vale. Hay que jerarquizar en un mundo en el que el tiempo es escaso y más vale dedicarlo a algo fruto del talento.[3]

Veamos ahora el caso concreto del mercado de un país pequeño como Uruguay, con poco más de tres millones de habitantes y con una gran concentración de la población en su capital, Montevideo. La ciudad cuenta con una buena red de distribución y de librerías, que intentan acomodar sus espacios a la enorme cantidad de novedades que surgen del propio país y del exterior. Pero son tantos los libros nuevos que aparecen, que la arquitectura de las librerías no puede contenerlos con facilidad. Las librerías en muchos casos deben especializarse, o simplemente ofrecer una selección de todo lo que se imprime, selección que casi nunca va dirigida a la calidad, si no a lo que se vende con más facilidad. Entonces: ¿Cómo destacar un título entre tantos? ¿Cómo conseguir espacios de prensa entre tanta oferta? ¿Cómo conseguir lugar en los escaparates de las librerías para mi producto? ¿Cómo hacer que mi libro se destaque frente al otro y al otro y al otro…?

Los demasiados libros crean confusión, un derroche de oferta para una demanda que no crece en la misma medida. Cito nuevamente a Jordi Nadal: "Demasiados títulos es una de las formas de censura, porque el exceso de información, el exceso de novedades, causa indiferencia. En este contexto, más no es mejor. Hay que abandonar el mito de la cantidad y abonar el de la calidad."[4] Este es entonces el panorama, el escenario que hemos tenido sobre el libro de papel en estos últimos años.

2. Tiempo, velocidad

El intercambio, el envío de mensajes, cartas (*e-mails*), textos, fotos, ideas, noticias e información, hoy es miles de veces más rápida que lo que nuestra generación hacía hace muy pocos años. No precisamos hablar de nuestros padres ni de nuestros abuelos para ejemplificar los cambios. Los avances tecnológicos se han producido en tan pocos años que nosotros mismos hemos sido los protagonistas. Hasta hace muy poco parecía que el día duraba veinticuatro horas enteras, todo marchaba más despacio de lo que parecen moverse las cosas hoy. La ansiedad, el apresuramiento por tener al instante los datos y la información que requerimos, han disminuido las oportunidades de observación, de investigación y análisis detallado. El cambio cultural que esto ha provocado nos ha vuelto impacientes en todas nuestras actividades. El ritmo acelerado en el cual vivimos incluye al comercio del libro.

Quisiera ahora recordar un típico intercambio entre la Librería Linardi y Risso y una biblioteca académica norteamericana, en este caso la universidad de Stanford, para ilustrar la forma serena con que sucedían las cosas entre los miembros del SALALM en los años previos al *e-mail*, hace muy poco tiempo. El recordado James Breedlove de la universidad de Stanford envió una carta fechada con el 9 de julio de 1992 interesándose en parte del archivo de la escritora Juana de Ibarborou. La orden de compra llegó el 28 de julio de 1992, y el primero de septiembre de 1992 le enviamos una carta anunciando la salida de los materiales. Todo demoró en hacerse casi dos meses. Con esta tranquila lentitud, manejábamos el negocio del libro hasta hace unos pocos años. Hoy las comunicaciones viajan a velocidad tal que nos inquietamos si en el mismo día—o en el lejano día siguiente—no recibimos respuesta a nuestros asuntos.

Vayamos ahora a Bogotá, abril de 2008. En el Segundo Congreso Iberoamericano de Libreros al cual fui invitado a participar, Antonio Ramírez propietario de la reconocida librería La Central de Barcelona resume muy bien nuestra actualidad en "Un lugar para la librería que viene," publicado en las memorias del segundo Congreso Iberoamericano de Libreros, Bogotá abril de 2008: "Si el tiempo de lo digital y lo global es el de la velocidad de lo inmediato, el tiempo del libro es el de la lentitud de la reflexión, de la sutil asimilación de una forma elocuente, la degustación pausada de un texto estable y finito."[5]

Estamos transitando una época en que Google nos responde casi todo, y sin esperas. La era de los demasiados libros está paulatinamente llegando a su fin, pues coincide con el crecimiento sostenido de la era digital. Los nuevos soportes como el *e-book*, serán el freno inevitable que detendrá los actuales excesos de la industria editorial. Los demasiados libros no podrán convivir con la explosión de la era digital, y estas dos corrientes chocarán como polos opuestos. Es razonable creer que los demasiados libros se reducirán a niveles sensatos y entraremos en el nuevo mundo del libro, un ineludible universo mixto donde los soportes tradicionales, de papel, y los modernos, digitales, deberán convivir. Los contenidos de internet y del libro electrónico servirán asimismo para depurar lo que se publica en papel y lo que se exhibe en librerías y otros puntos de venta. Los primeros cambios significativos ya los hemos visto con la desaparición de las grandes enciclopedias de varios volúmenes que se editaban hasta hace pocos años.

Los innumerables sitios web donde podemos consultar todo tipo de información, están transformando los métodos tradicionales del conocimiento. Los dispositivos de lectura de *e-book*, ya sea el Kindle o el Sony Reader o el iPad, nos están ofreciendo una fiesta a la cual no hemos sido invitados, aunque debemos participar en ella. Esta transformación tecnológica no pertenece al mundo cultural ni al mundo intelectual, sino que es promovida por los fabricantes de artículos electrónicos.

Este nuevo camino no se debe a una demanda de los lectores ni de los profesionales del libro; son los vendedores de dispositivos electrónicos quienes quieren imponer sus productos en el mercado. El consumismo y el esnobismo por las innovaciones tecnológicas, tienen muchos adeptos siempre dispuestos a poseer el último modelo de algún novedoso aparato. Pero en esta fiesta de la tecnología: ¿Podemos los profesionales del libro estar ausentes o indiferentes a estos cambios? Por supuesto que no.

Tenemos la certeza de que, como ha afirmado Pablo Arrieta en *Sobre los libros por venir: un menú de opciones*, "el libro tradicional no va a ser reemplazado del todo por otra tecnología. Lo que pasa es que la familia de soportes, formas y su difusión se ha ampliado. Y lo importante es aprender a descubrir sus bondades y diferencias, para que coexistan y se alimenten para bien."[6]

También pensamos que la auténtica verdad sobre el futuro del libro tradicional, se conocerá cuando la generación de nativos digitales desplace totalmente a las generaciones de inmigrantes digitales. Allí es cuando se podrá apreciar el lugar exacto que le va a corresponder al libro de papel.

3. El mundo mixto como idea del futuro

Al mirar hacia adelante, hay muchas preguntas y dudas que tenemos con relación a lo que se viene para el libro. Lo dijimos al principio de esta charla: no disponemos de muchas certezas, más bien podemos percibir, vislumbrar, tener sospechas de algunos acontecimientos que pueden suceder. La informática no nos da todas las respuestas y renueva nuestras incertidumbres. ¿Cómo controlaremos la venta de los libros electrónicos? ¿Cómo protegeremos el trabajo de los editores, libreros y autores?

Los riesgos que implican la digitalización del libro son muchos y los derechos de autor son y serán una gran dificultad para su correcto desarrollo. Las facilidades que otorga el mundo digital para la copia y reproducción de textos, perturba y preocupa a la industria del libro, y es aquí donde los autores podrán jugar un papel importante en la protección de sus ingresos. El soporte digital es un recurso óptimo para la piratería y la reproducción ilegal, ya que no existen controles eficaces para las descargas de internet. En la web no hay que pagar prácticamente nada, y se ha hecho costumbre que la música, las películas y el software se bajen gratis de internet, lo que nos muestra una experiencia que pone en riesgo el comercio del libro.

Pero asimismo, ¿en dónde y en qué guardaremos nuestros archivos? Todavía no se ha inventado ningún soporte que sea más confiable y durable que el papel. ¿Qué métodos de conservación tan buenos como el papel ofrece el mundo digital? ¿A dónde llegarán todos estos cambios? ¿Qué podemos predecir en este sentido?

El mundo mixto es la idea más interesante de mirar el futuro. Asistiremos a un nuevo tiempo donde convivirán las nuevas tecnologías y el libro tradicional en papel. En el nuevo mundo mixto, la impresión por demanda será la encargada de mantener en existencia todos los ejemplares que sean comercializados, sin necesidad de ocupar espacios físicos en los depósitos, y sin tirajes sobrantes que terminen elevando los precios de venta. La Espresso Book Machine y otras máquinas por el estilo, nos harán la impresión por demanda en pocos minutos.

La reciente encuesta de consumo cultural efectuada en Uruguay en 2009, arrojó como resultado que el 20 por ciento de los lectores de libros obtuvo el último libro que leyó por un regalo que le realizaron. Mundialmente, se calcula que en promedio, el 25 por ciento de los libros que se venden, son utilizados para regalar. Comprar un libro como regalo es una práctica usual para todos nosotros.

Si el libro se transforma totalmente en electrónico, ¿qué podríamos regalar? ¿Una descarga de internet? ¿Cómo se vería un libro objeto, un libro de arte, de arquitectura, diseño, de fotografía en formato digital? ¿Cómo se verá un *coffee table book* en formato digital? No todos los libros serán adecuados para ser publicados solamente en formatos digitales.

Para finalizar esta presentación queremos decir que nos encontramos ante un momento histórico en el universo del libro, marcado por dos grandes acontecimientos, dos grandes tendencias: por un lado los demasiados libros y por el otro el libro electrónico y digital. Creemos que la edición industrializada y globalizada de hoy, dará paso, lentamente, al mundo mixto de mañana, en donde el libro tradicional en papel sobrevivirá. Nunca será reemplazado totalmente.

La combinación de todas las oportunidades disponibles convertirán al futuro libro en un producto más complejo y variado, más diverso. Todas estas posibilidades, funcionando conjuntamente, serán los libros de mañana.

NOTAS

1. Zaid, *Los demasiados libros*, 11–12.
2. Ibid., 19–20.
3. Nadal y García, *Libros o velocidad*, 1.
4. Ibid., x.
5. CERLALC, *Memorias*, 156. Disponible en http://www.cerlalc.org/secciones/libro_desarrollo/Memorias_II_Congreso_Libreros.pdf.
6. Ibid., 174.

BIBLIOGRAFÍA

Centro Regional para el Fomento del Libro en América Latina, el Caribe y Portugal-CERLALC. *Memorias: segundo Congreso Iberoamericano de Libreros: pensar la librería como espacio cultural.* Bogotá: CERLALC, 2009.

Nadal, Jordi y Francisco García. *Libros o velocidad: reflexiones sobre el oficio editorial.* México: Fondo de Cultura Económica, 2005.

Zaid, Gabriel. *Los demasiados libros.* Barcelona: Editorial Anagrama, 1996.

3. Don't Try to Change Them: How SALALM's History Provides Insight into the Future of Latin American Studies Library Development

Mark L. Grover

In June 1956 librarians from several U.S. institutions met together for the first Seminar on the Acquisition of Latin American Library Materials (SALALM) at Chinsegut Hill, near the town of Brooksville, Florida. Challenges related to the Farmington Plan motivated librarians to come together to talk about the issues involved in building large and comprehensive collections on Latin America. The sixteen working papers presented at the seminar examined many aspects of selecting, ordering, and acquiring materials from Latin America. The meeting was deemed a success and a second meeting was held at the University of Texas at Austin the following year. A permanent organization was formed with a primary purpose of exploring challenges librarians face in building, processing, and servicing a library collection of materials about Latin America.[1]

Today in 2010 we meet again in somewhat similar circumstances. Libraries in the United States are experiencing significant difficulties related to budgetary restraints and the changing nature of our profession. These challenges are affecting our abilities and resolve to build collections of Latin American library materials. Though the concerns are different than those of our predecessors in 1956, the issues are the same, how to build collections that support the curriculum and research needs of our students and faculty. The history of SALALM is an impressive story of librarians, publishers, and bookdealers working together to establish methods and procedures enabling us to accomplish our goals and aspirations. Within these fifty-four years of successes and occasional failures, lessons have been learned. Those lessons should serve as a guide not only to us but particularly our library and university administrators as we navigate this interesting and challenging time. We as librarians, who work on the front lines of both the research world and the Latin American book trade, need to remember that our primary goal continues to be to service the needs of our patrons and not succumb to the occasional questionable demands of university and library administrators.

The purpose of this paper is to briefly examine one early important SALALM experience related to acquiring Latin American books for our

19

libraries. The Latin American Cooperative Acquisition Program (LACAP) was a centralized acquisition program established by U.S. libraries connected to SALALM and an American book company that began in 1960 and continued to 1972. The lessons learned from this experiment bring into question the ability of large U.S. companies with broad region-based acquisition objectives to succeed when compared to small in-country dealers. The lessons learned influenced the methods we presently use for acquisition and should help us appreciate the current challenges involved in identifying, acquiring, and processing library materials from Latin America. Though the library and publishing worlds are changing, there are certain cultural aspects of the Latin American book trade that remain constant.

SALALM and Latin American Acquisitions

The first SALALM meeting in 1956 provides an interesting introduction to American librarians and their/our approach to Latin America. There were some thoughtful and informative working papers that presented basic information on how to identify and acquire library materials. The focus of most of the papers, however, was on the frustrations librarians were having. The underlying message was that the Latin American publishing and distribution system was archaic, complicated, and unresponsive. Most of the papers included examples of the difficulty American librarians had with the Latin American book culture. The papers had a theme of superiority suggesting that the Latin American system needed to change to become something with which Americans could work. That tone was emphasized by Fermín Peraza, director of the Municipal Library of Havana, Cuba, when he suggested the need for cooperation between the Americas:

> Looking toward the future, not heeding territorial frontiers, forgetting the differences of races and customs, we should like to see the Americas united in the aim of bettering their institutions; and...directing themselves especially towards Latin America; inviting it to take part in the paramount struggle for culture, and stop dying in its own blood, maddened by hate and local resentments.[2]

One exception to that theme was a paper by Emma Crosland Simonson from the University of California at Berkeley. Responding to negativity towards Latin America, Simonson focused on the necessity of understanding Latin America and maintaining a positive approach to the process of acquiring materials. "There has been a long history of pessimism on the subject of Latin American purchases. It is customary to bewail the lack of selection tools, the non-response from Latin American firms, and the large percentage of failure in receiving requested material." She suggested that the responsibility for a successful acquisitions program lay with the library. Instead of complaining, changes should be made in U.S. libraries to improve the process. The most essential prerequisite was to learn about the Latin American book world. She strongly advocated that librarians go to Latin America and become familiar with the cultural history of the region. "It will more than justify the expense involved. Aside from the economy in book costs, the increase in better relations for future activity will be worth this expenditure." She suggested learning the culture of business in Latin America and conforming to their system instead of expecting Latin Americans to change. Her final advice was pertinent: "Finally, we too often forget that our dealings with Latin America is a two-way business. We tend to plan and think in our terms only. We cannot do that and succeed. We have to remember their problems, their lack of mass production methods, and most important of all, that their life is not geared to the cult of business efficiency."[3]

For SALALM's next several meetings, the primary focus of the discussions was on issues of acquisition. It was not always negative but universally demonstrated a frustration with the challenges U.S. librarians experienced working in Latin America. By the fourth meeting SALALM librarians determined to do something. The answer was to develop a program with a private U.S. company to identify and purchase Latin American materials for U.S. libraries.

SALALM and LACAP

The primary challenges American librarians faced were that the Latin American book trade was focused internally, and that the ability of librarians in the United States to obtain recently published materials was problematic. For librarians in the United States, just determining what was being published in Latin America was difficult. That challenge was exacerbated by the difficulty in finding a dealer or bookstore in Latin America willing to supply those materials. In addition, the large number of countries in Latin America frustrated librarians.

During a social gathering at the fourth SALALM meeting held in Washington, D.C., in 1959, an outline of a cooperative project was developed. As the head of the New York Public Library stated to Nettie Lee Benson, Latin American Studies librarian at the University of Texas, "We have talked about it for four years but we haven't made any progress."[4]

The plan was simple. A private book company, Stechert-Hafner centered in New York City, would employ traveling agents throughout Latin America to identify recent academic publications and purchase multiple copies of those materials. Librarians would provide to Stechert-Hafner general subject outlines of their collection needs and agree to purchase the item selected for them under what is commonly known as a "blanket order" agreement. Knowing the collecting needs of each library, traveling agents would determine the number of books to purchase based on the profiles provided. Stechert-Hafner agreed to initially finance the venture with the goal of breaking even within three years.

This program was particularly attractive to American libraries because they only had to work with one company to build their collections.[5]

The project was administered by Dominick Coppola from Stechert-Hafner. Nettie Lee Benson and Coppola were the first traveling agents. Ms. Benson took a six-month unpaid leave of absence from the University of Texas and traveled to Venezuela, Colombia, Ecuador, Peru, Chile, and Bolivia between January and May of 1960. Her adventures are delightfully described in typical Dr. Benson fashion highlighting the joys, challenges, and intrigue of buying books in Latin America. Between March and May of the same year, Coppola visited Central America and Mexico. Books selected and purchased by Benson and Coppola were in U.S. libraries by the summer of 1960. Dr. Benson took two additional trips: January to July 1961 to the rest of the Spanish-speaking countries of South America, and April to July 1962 to Central America and a return visit to four of the countries she visited in 1960.[6]

Brazil was the last major country added to the program. The hesitancy about going into Brazil was related to the size and complexity of the book trade. By May 1963 they were ready, and Dr. A. W. Bork of Southern Illinois University visited Brazil. He immediately recognized the geographical challenges that made the acquisition of books from Brazil difficult. In most countries of Latin America, LACAP could obtain most of the desired academic material by working out of the capital city. The vastness and strong regionalism of Brazil made that impossible. The decision was made to establish a permanent office for LACAP in Rio de Janeiro administered by a Brazilian academic, Vicente Barretto.[7]

What became clear to LACAP administrators was that Latin America had not one book trade but many. Each country had unique and different book cultures. The administrators of the program at Stechert-Hafner realized that in order to maintain adequate control and to understand the publication industry in each country, they needed someone in the country. A traveling agent who visited once a year was not adequate particularly in the larger countries. Stechert-Hafner determined that fact early and established permanent representatives in several places in Latin America.[8]

The program struggled for many years. The goal of becoming self-sufficient was never reached. The cost involved for a company headquartered in the United States with representatives throughout the region was prohibitive. Latin America was large with too many countries to make it cost-effective to provide what U.S. libraries wanted. At the end of 1972, Stechert-Hafner discontinued LACAP.[9]

The primary reason LACAP failed was because of competition from Latin American companies. What LACAP did by purchasing large quantities of library materials in Latin America was to impress upon a few dealers that there was a large enough library market in the United States to make a successful business. By the late 1960s, dealers from most of the major countries had begun competing with LACAP. They were able to better determine what was being published and sell books at more affordable prices. That initial small number of Latin American bookdealers has expanded to the present time when more than forty Latin American companies work with the international market primarily in the United States. They function similarly to the way LACAP did; they determine new books and periodicals that are available in the country, offer "approval programs," make lists, send those lists to libraries in North America and Europe, and sell the identified books at the cost of the book plus a fee, which is incorporated into the price of the book.[10]

LACAP was an important experiment for SALALM because it taught us the difficulty and cost involved for U.S. companies working in Latin America. We had the illusion we could succeed because of motivation and superior business methods. We quickly learned that Latin American dealers who were in country and understood the culture could better provide what we needed at a lower cost. Over our fifty-four-year history, SALALM has been good at identifying challenges in the selection and acquisition of materials from Latin America. We have been successful in developing programs related to American library research, referencing, and processing. Occasionally as in the case of LACAP, we have tried programs where we got directly involved in the book market and library world in Latin America. We have learned over and over that we cannot do it on our own. Our success has come from working with Latin Americans, not trying to change the system. Probably our best success has been to encourage a corps of competent, small, effective, and responsive dealers who understand our needs and are able to work in each country's book market.

Current Challenges

The constant historical dilemma of libraries is adjusting to change. When those changes involve the international book market, the challenges are more difficult and complex. We need to continually remind ourselves of a couple of obvious principles that occasionally are forgotten by librarians in the United States. The first is that the Latin American publishing world is focused on the local and in-country demands, not the international market. This is especially true with the academic publishing industry. It is controlled by local universities, agencies, institutes, and governments. The international library market is so small and insignificant that our needs or desires have little impact on the industry. The obvious consequence is that we are required to work within the culture, customs, and regulations of each Latin American country and not expect the market to adjust to our demands.

A second aspect is that the type of materials needed for our research collections do not mirror the books that populate the bookstores of Latin America. We do not build successful research library collections by mimicking capital cities' bookstore collections. The materials needed for our patrons are generally research publications generated by foundations, institutes, governmental agencies, university presses, and private publishers. Regional materials are often more important than publications that will sell in the bookstores of the large cities. Consequently, the logistical and cultural challenges involved in obtaining these materials can be complicated. Though the introduction of digital publishing is making access to some of these materials less problematic, particularly government documents, it continues to be a challenge to get the desired materials.

The financial and cultural reality is that we must have dealers in country to ensure adequate coverage. These dealers are familiar with the publishing market, the university cultures, government and institute publishing, and local customs. They establish contacts and connections that are impossible for American librarians to do. They equally have to be familiar with us as their clients. They have to know how American universities function as well as our curriculum and research practices and methods. They have to understand American/European business practices and regulations. They are intermediators who are familiar with both cultures.

As a historian I have often recognized the similarities between the way our dealers function and that of the translators and mediators between the conquistadores and native populations in the colonial past of the Americas. Notice how the description of this historical figure fits the role of the bookdealer:

> Moving across these frontiers demanded extraordinary skill. Intermediaries became repositories of two or more cultures; they changed roles at will in accordance with circumstances. Of necessity, their lives reflected a complexity unknown to those living within the confines of a single culture. They knew how the "other side" thought and behaved, and they responded accordingly. Their grasp of different perspectives led all sides to value them, although not all may have trusted them. Often they walked through a network of interconnections where they alone brought some understanding among disparate peoples. These mediators therefore have held a distinct position in our past and into the present.[11]

We as librarians have a similar role as translators or mediators between Latin America and our university community, particularly administrators. Our positions exist because to build a collection of Latin American materials requires unique skills and knowledge. Our primary responsibility is to ensure that the research and curriculum needs of our faculty and students are met. We have a significant responsibility not only as facilitators for the library patrons but as informants and educators to our library administration about the way the publishing industry functions in Latin America. This responsibility is becoming increasingly more crucial as the divide between the publishing and research world and the mind-set of university administrators becomes wider. This role for us is important because of the rapidly changing nature of librarianship in the United States compared to the different and slower rate of change occurring in the Latin American publishing world. We often find ourselves having to instruct and caution our library and university administrators, because their expectations are related to changes occurring here in the United States and not in Latin America.

The time in which we live is confusing. The availability of so much information in digital format combined with soothsayers predicting the end of the book suggests fundamental changes in the way scholarship, publishing, and research occur. The promises of a paperless society, access to all documents in digital forms, and disappearing libraries and librarians are attractive ideas to many university administrators. The problem is that legitimate research on the reality of what is happening does not support the prophecies of those predicting massive changes. Those studies seem to have limited effect on administrators who are thrilled with the predictions of complete digitized libraries because it is a way to save money and space. The reality is that books continue to be used and published at a higher rate, publishers still struggle to make money with e-books, methods of digital delivery are still not satisfactory, and much of the quality research and published materials are not likely to become available in digital format without costs. In some ways administrators are trying to drain the tub as we are getting ready to take a bath, hoping that just getting our feet wet is equivalent to a full bath of the past.

The title of my presentation, "Don't Try to Change Them," is a caution to us as librarians to not forget that we work with a book and publishing culture that is strong and established. My ideas are based on examining fifty-four years of experience SALALM has had with Latin America. As we approach the challenges of our time, I suggest the following:

1. We need to realize that as librarians from the United States we have virtually no influence or ability to change the Latin American system. No matter how much we want all books to be available in digital format, it will only occur when the Latin American market and academic world want it to happen. The only way to work with Latin America is to determine how best to function within their system.

2. The most important influence we can have at the present time is to ensure that our administrators and faculty appreciate what is happening. Our administrators live and function in a United States cultural environment, and it is understandable that they want everything internationally to function in a way that fits their needs. Though they may want change, we have to accept Latin America as it is and not try to transform it. When we work with them, it has to be based on the way Latin America functions not on how we want it to function. An interesting and informative example of this is Darlene Hull's story of a major American distributor's attempt to work in the Dominican Republic. They pulled out because they kept insisting on changes in

bureaucratic processing procedures and were unwilling to make their own adjustments.[12]

3. We need to recognize that the primary function of our dealers is to identify and provide research materials. The last thing that we want is to base decisions on where we purchase materials on peripheral services that may be desired. We need to understand what they do best which is to identify and supply the best and the latest research materials. Do not make them catalogers or processors just because it saves us a few cents. My fear is that we will encourage what I have called the "Walmartinization" of the book trade just so we can have unimportant and insignificant services that are available from dealers in the United States. We have traditionally found that smaller operations within a country have been able to provide the personalized service better than larger more commercial companies.

4. We need to recognize the importance and value of our dealers in providing information that helps us with decisions related to our libraries. They are partners with us. They are on the front lines and know what is happening. At the same time we need to make sure we do not allow our dealers to become lazy. Their value is that they do not only deal with the easy and simple. We need to keep up on all that is happening to ensure they are doing what we need.

5. While attempting to maintain a semblance of the reality of what is happening in Latin America, it is also important for us recognize that changes will occur and we need to be ready. As Dror Faust from Puvill has suggested:

> In order to reverse the movement toward the loss of cohesion, book dealers and librarians must act together. We must focus on presenting bold new alternatives for overcoming today's obstacles. The problem is not about the fate of Latin American librarianship. Rather, the challenge is to use our shared experiences, our collective knowledge, partnership, and leadership to build new avenues for enhancing collections with cost-saving features, which will constitute a model for library administrators to follow in other areas.[13]

6. We as Latin Americanist librarians have to continue to spend time in Latin America. It is important that we walk the streets of Latin America to constantly reinforce our understanding of what is happening. We need to visit bookstores, publishers, universities, and research institutes. We need to go to book fairs. By so doing we maintain an appreciation of the culture of the book trade, how things function, and what is changing. No matter how fast information travels on the Internet or how good it is, we cannot understand or appreciate a country without being there to observe, appreciate, and enjoy.

Conclusion

This is an exhilarating time to be a librarian. The potential that technological advances offer our profession is exciting. My caution is that we continue to recognize that there is not a universal change occurring, particularly in the third world. My worry is that decisions in our libraries will be made based on false expectations that will hinder and hurt the study of Latin America at our universities. The lessons we have learned from the history of SALALM suggest that librarians in conjunction with our colleagues in Latin America, particularly our bookdealers, will be able to navigate the next few years to preserve the fundamental elements of our profession.

NOTES

1. SALALM is an international organization with participants from around the world, but most members are from the United States. For a description of the first meeting, see Mark L. Grover, "The Beginning of SALALM," in *Latin American Studies Research and Bibliography: Past, Present, and Future,* ed. Pamela F. Howard-Reguindin (New Orleans: SALALM Secretariat, 2007), 16–42.

2. Fermín Peraza, "Which Are the Latin American Books United States Libraries Need," *SALALM 1,* Working Paper No. II e 3, pp. 2, 5, 12.

3. Emma Crosland Simonson, "Purchase of Latin American Materials through Bookstores, Publishers and Dealers," *SALALM 1,* Working Paper No. II e 2, pp. 1, 7, 9.

4. Nettie Lee Benson, interview by William Jackson, n.d., Austin, Texas, original in possession of William Jackson.

5. M. J. Savary, *The Latin American Cooperative Acquisitions Program: An Imaginative Venture* (New York: Hafner Publishing, 1968), 54–57.

6. For a description of her trips, see Nettie Lee Benson, "Report of the Latin American Cooperative Acquisition Project," in *Seminar on the Acquisition of Latin American Library Materials, V, New York City, June 14–16, 1960. Final Report and Working Papers* (Washington, D.C.: Pan American Union, 1965), 263–84; and Nettie Lee Benson, "LACAP Report Number Two," Seminar on the Acquisition of Latin American Library Materials, VI, Southern Illinois University, Carbondale, Ill., July 6–8, 1961, Working Papers (unpublished), copy found in the SALALM Archives, Benson Library, University of Texas at Austin. See also letters written from South America found in her papers at the University of Texas, Benson Latin American Library Archives, Nettie Lee Benson Collection, Box NLB Office Files-BLAC info.

7. See his report, Albert William Bork, "LACAP Survey in Brazil," in *Seminar on the Acquisition of Latin American Library Materials, VIII, Madison, Wisconsin, July 11–12, 1963. Final Report and Working Papers,* 2 vols. (Washington, D.C.: Pan American Union, 1964), 136–50.

8. For a pessimistic evaluation of LACAP, see "Resources for Research in Latin American Literature in Southern Libraries," in *Essays in Hispanic Bibliography,* by Lawrence S. Thompson (Hamden, Conn.: Shoe String Press, 1970), 100–1.

9. Laura Gutierrez-Witt and Donald L. Gibbs, "Acquiring Latin American Books," *Library Acquisitions: Practice and Theory* 6 (1982): 168–69.

10. The speed at which books are cataloged and made available to U.S. scholars was noted by the Mexican scholar Federico Patán in an article suggesting that Mexican books were processed faster in United States libraries than in Mexican libraries. Federico Patán, "Mexicanos en una computadora," *Uno más uno,* suplemento *Sábado,* June 17, 1995, p. 10. For a list of most

of the companies working with U.S. libraries, see the SALALM home page, http://salalm.org/booksellers/vendorcontactinfo/.

11. Margaret Connell Szasz, ed., *Between Indian and White Worlds: The Cultural Broker* (Norman: University of Oklahoma Press, 1994), 6.

12. Darlene Hull-Grullón, "The Future Isn't What It Used to Be: Can We Hang onto the Best of the Old and Merge It with the New?" (Paper presented at the Seminar on the Acquisition of Latin American Library Materials LIV, Berlin, Germany, July 3–8, 2009).

13. Dror Faust, "A Book Dealer's Perspective on the Crisis in Latin Americanist Libraries," *SALALM Newsletter* 37 (December 2009): 104.

4. The Truth That No One Wants to Know: Preserving the Record of Unprecedented Violence in Ciudad Juárez, 2008–Present

Molly Molloy

In late June 2010, I gave a presentation about the homicide numbers in Ciudad Juárez at the National Association of Hispanic Journalists (NAHJ) meeting in Denver. I had just said that the number of people killed in Juárez (as of June 24) was more than fifty-seven hundred, and I had provided documentation of how I got those numbers. Not five minutes later, another speaker on the panel, an editor with a major worldwide news service, said the number was "almost fifty-five hundred."

As happens over and over in the reporting on the violence in Ciudad Juárez, the most violent city in the world, several hundred people are erased from the count of the dead. We should note that in most of the years before 2007, the total number of people murdered in Juárez in a year generally hovered between two hundred and three hundred, so the number left out of the current count by the editor speaking on the panel was as many or more than the entire annual number of people killed in the city for most of the previous fifteen years or more.

In part, it is this tendency in the press and by many academics, to downplay the violence in Juárez that exploded in January 2008 and continues to spiral upwards, that has inspired me to keep a daily count and to inform as many journalists, academics, and activists as possible about the human rights disaster unfolding in Juárez and that is now spreading to other places in Mexico. What I would like to share with you today are a few more personal accounts of what covering this story is like and to demonstrate how important it is to preserve this record for the future.

The death count begins in Juárez on January 1, 2008. The year 2007 had been the most violent in the recent history of the city—more than three hundred people were murdered. By the end of 2008, the murder toll reached 1,623. In 2009, the newspapers reported 2,660 deaths by homicide in the city, though a later report from the state attorney general's office said the total number of murder victims was 2,754, and that the Juárez morgue had performed 2,626 autopsies that year—one every 2.5 hours. As of September 14, 2010, more than 2,180 people have been victims of homicide in the city of Juárez this year—a city of less than 1.2 million people.

This death toll includes fifteen people who attended a birthday party where, just after midnight on January 31, an armed commando blocked off the narrow street in the Villas de Salvárcar neighborhood and entered three adjacent small homes shooting everyone as they ran from the barrage of automatic rifle fire. Early that Sunday morning, stories appeared on the online site of *El Diario de Juárez* reporting that thirteen young people had been slaughtered (an additional two later died in the hospital), and I wrote to a list of email correspondents:

> I should label this one: "why I am not a Christian..." These stories were posted this morning at about 10 am, but I was on my way out to play music at a church in Las Cruces. The sermon and scripture today was all about LOVE—St. Paul's Letter to the Corinthians, chapter 13, verses 1–13.... Many of you probably know it by heart like I do.

The online newspaper displays the photographs. Rivers of blood in the street outside of the house. A rubber glove dropped in a pool of blood by an emergency worker. The empty room, a boombox against the wall where the partiers had been dancing, the floor now red with blood—still wet, sticky, and dark. As St. Paul wrote in 1 Corinthians 13:12: "For now we see through a glass, darkly; but then face to face: now I know in part; but then shall I know even as also I am known."

The massacre of the students in Villas de Salvárcar was seen as a turning point in the violent life of Juárez—mainly because government officials from the president on down immediately jumped on the "they were gangsters working for one cartel killed by gangsters working for another cartel" bandwagon, and then had to eat their words. The only reason the officials did not get away with the "dead therefore guilty therefore dead" version of crime-solving this time is that mothers of the dead kids stood up and said, "*basta!*"

That does not happen often in Juárez. In most of the murder cases, even the mass murders, the explanation is always that those killed were members of gangs working for drug cartels and so only the bad people—*los malandros*—are dead. The mayor of Juárez made a statement in June 2008 after some five hundred people had already been murdered that "only five innocent civilians" were among the victims. After more than sixty-five hundred murders in the city since January 2008, he still maintains that only some two hundred of them are innocent bystanders. In April, President Felipe Calderón gave a speech to business leaders in the tourism sector and said that "less than 10 percent of murder victims were innocent bystanders or police or soldiers killed in the line of duty" and that more than 90 percent of the dead are criminals killed by other criminals.[1]

Even better is Calderón's exchange with Wolf Blitzer on CNN during his U.S. visit in May 2010:

> BLITZER: Because I—I'm wondering, are the drug gangs, the cartels, are they winning this war right now? When I hear a number like twenty-three thousand people killed since you launched your initiative…
>
> CALDERÓN: No. They—they are not winning. Let me clarify that the other part of my answer. Most of that—90 percent of those casualties are of— are casualties of criminals themselves that are fighting each other. It's very clear for us according—with our records, that it's possible to understand, for instance, in one particular homicide, what could be the probable reasons for that, and 90 percent of that are criminals linked in one way or another to the gangs. Now, the Mexican gangs are passing through a very unstable process, splitting themselves and fighting each other. That explains most of those casualties. They are not—
>
> BLITZER: These are not innocent civilians among the twenty-three thousand?
>
> CALDERÓN: Some of them.
>
> BLITZER: You're saying that many of them are gang members themselves?
>
> CALDERÓN: Ninety percent.
>
> BLITZER: Ninety percent?
>
> CALDERÓN: Ninety percent, yes. Ninety percent out of all of the homicides that we are able to understand or explain the causes of that. Two percent of that, less than 2 percent are innocent civilians, yes, more or less killed by the criminals. That's the worst part of that.[2]

Yet, the death toll never stops rising, less than 1 percent of the crimes are investigated, and the dead become de facto drug war criminals due to the simple fact that they have been murdered. Academics and government pundits give statements to the press filled with vague interpretations of certain "messages" that they say indicate that the dead are members of organized crime. Perpetrators are seldom caught and when they are caught, their "guilt" is determined by the confessions they give after being beaten by police. Nothing is ever proven with evidence in a court of law that we would recognize. The guilty are dead and they are dead because they are guilty. A foolproof and economical system of justice.

The headline a few days after the massacre at Villas de Salvárcar said one of the killers had asked about separating out the women and children, but the commando leader said, "No, give it to them all the same." A few days later, a forty-three-year-old mother whose only two sons were murdered in the massacre, faced down the president of Mexico at a public meeting:

> "Excuse me, Mr. President, but I will not shake your hand because you are not my friend. I cannot welcome you, because as far as I am concerned, you

are not welcome here....For me, there is no justice. All I have are two dead sons. I want you to put yourself in my place....It is not fair that my boys are at a party and are killed. I want you to apologize for what you have said, that they were gangsters. It is a lie!"[3]

When I first sat down to write this piece, the Villas de Salvárcar massacre and the mother's passionate speech to the president were to be the emotional center of this essay. But early the very next morning, the headline in *El Diario* read, "Massacre at Wake: Six Killed." The Juárez website lapolaka.com called it, "Replica of Villas de Salvárcar." As it turns out, six people were shot dead as they ran from the house in the Praderas del Sur neighborhood that Thursday night while attending the wake for an eighteen-year-old boy who had been murdered the previous Tuesday. It seems he might have tried to undercut a junkyard syndicate by selling stolen car parts. His family tried to report something to the police and they were threatened and then slaughtered at the wake. Two more people, women of grandmotherly age—the stalwarts of any Mexican *velorio*—later died in the hospital.[4]

By midday, the massacred mourners of Praderas del Sur had disappeared from the news, perhaps because they were poorer people, perhaps because of fear of being associated with the family, or fear that it would also happen to silenced neighbors and witnesses. Silence ruled that Friday. Then *Lapolaka* posted another story headlined, "Videogames for the kids." They line up at a chain-link fence. Others sit on the ground a few feet away from a body lying under a piece of rotten plywood and a white painted door with a brass knob. Beside them, a yellow dog watches and a police photographer dressed in black goes about his work. The man had been assassinated in the act of stealing the door that now lay across his body.[5]

I would ask the government officials who chant the "cartel war" mantra exactly why a drug cartel criminal would steal a door from an abandoned house and get murdered for it. This is how most of the killings go down in Juárez: one small article, or just a line or two in an article in the morning newspaper that sums up the six, eight, ten, or a dozen killings that happened the day before. The majority of the dead by far are the poor people of the city, looking for some way to survive in an economy that gives them few legitimate options.

The next day, a Saturday, I checked the news in the early afternoon and noted that two people were shot to death at point-blank range in their car very close to the downtown office of the mayor of Juárez, almost directly under the Paso del Norte bridge leading to El Paso. This was how *Lapolaka* told the story:

In the middle of Hell, God is Great...!

A baby survived the bullets of organized crime during a brutal execution with AK-47s in the heart of the city. The little girl was uninjured in the rain of lead, but not so her young parents who died at her side, riddled with bullets at the hands of the killers. The events took place during a spectacular chase…the family drove a Toyota SUV with Texas plates along the Heroico Colegio Militar highway. At the intersection of Cinco de Mayo, a commando pulled up to them and began to fire at them as they tried to escape. The driver of the Toyota lost control of the vehicle which then hit three other cars until finally crashing to a stop just behind the municipal government building. There, the man and woman were finished off by the gunmen who then fled. The baby was crying in her car seat without knowing what had happened, but uninjured despite the rain of bullets.[6]

It was not until around noon the next day that the national and world media reported that these victims were Americans, a man and his wife, who was an employee of the largest U.S. Consulate in the world in Ciudad Juárez. Almost the same moment, the Mexican husband of another consular worker was gunned down in another part of the city. His two children were injured, but survived. The picture of the two young American parents, shot through the head in the front seat of their car with the international bridge looming in the background, appeared in newspapers all over the world. These were not the first Americans killed in the border violence, but because of their connections to the government, these killings were noticed by presidents, cabinet secretaries, and most Americans who until this point had perhaps never heard of Ciudad Juárez, the most violent city in the world, just across the river from El Paso, Texas, one of the least violent cities in the United States.

Back in August 2008, I visited the site of what at that time was the largest mass murder in the recent history of Ciudad Juárez—nine people were killed in a drug rehab center during a church service. I was there some forty hours after the killings while the people who ran the center were trying to leave Juárez. They had been warned and they were preparing to close the place down and flee, but they did not get out in time. One of their first acts on the morning after the massacre was to whitewash the emblem of their group that had adorned the front of the small stucco building in the poor barrio. They could hardly work fast enough as they feared the gunmen could return—though this was a crime scene, there were no police, no soldiers standing guard, not even a shred of yellow crime scene tape. The blood was mostly mopped up, leaving only a few smeared handprints on the tile wall of the room where it happened. Flies were buzzing and clustering where blood had soaked into the cracks between the tiles. A red candle burned in the corner where the bodies had piled up. Taped to the wall, above the candle, was a piece of paper printed with the faded words of "The Serenity Prayer," a simple message that has inspired generations of addicts all over the world as they seek recovery. In the kitchen of the small house next door, a wake was being held for one of the victims, a nineteen-year-old gang member who had gone to the rehab center to try to break his glue-sniffing habit.[7]

The nine people who died that day in August 2008 were added to the total of 228 people killed that month—the highest monthly toll that year. A year later in August 2009, 316 people were murdered, a record broken in August 2010 when 336 people were killed in a single month. On September 2, 2009, the Casa Aliviane rehabilitation center was attacked and eighteen people were murdered. Then on September 15, the eve of Mexican Independence Day, ten more people were shot to death at the center called Anexo La Vida (Life Annex). Government officials have said that drug sellers and gang members were using the centers as hiding places. The killers used military gear and tactics. Most of the victims were young men from very poor families. Another rehab center in Chihuahua City was attacked in early June 2010 and at least nineteen people were killed in that massacre. Six more people were killed outside of a rehab clinic in Juárez on June 16, 2010.

People ask why I pay so much attention to counting the dead. What about the reasons for so much slaughter? What about social programs? My simple answer is that there are many reasons and I do not know them all, nor do I know of any short- or medium-term social programs that could stem the extreme violence that has become normal daily life for the people of the city. I can look at the victims though, the large majority of them ordinary and poor people with no obvious connections to the high-level cartels that are supposed to be at war, and know that the explanations given by the powerful and their mouthpieces do not fit with the evidence before my eyes. I tend to fall back on the answer given by one of the men cleaning up the first rehab center in August 2008. I asked him what was happening in Ciudad Juárez. His answer was simple: "Something evil. Something very, very evil."

It is evil that the several hundred thousand people still lucky enough to have a job in a foreign-owned factory in Juárez earn perhaps fifty dollars per week in a city where the cost of living is nearly as high as in the United States. It is evil that on the west side of the city, home to half a million people, there is only one public high school and that education beyond the ninth grade is not free. It is evil that in the past two years more than ten thousand orphans have been created by the official War on Drugs. It is evil that a young mother who fled across the border in April with her four children says, "all the children, the only thing they know how to play is *sicarios,*" which is the Spanish word for hired killers.[8]

Since January 2008, more than sixty-five hundred people have been killed in Juárez—an average of more than six murders per day. Juárez is now the most violent city in the world with a murder rate approaching 250 per 100,000 inhabitants. El Paso is one of the safest cities in the United States, with less than twenty murders per year.

Some people insist that my focus on the numbers denies the humanity of the victims and of those working for social change in Juárez. I disagree. The actual victims of the slaughter happening in Juárez disappear in the pages of commentary and policy analysis from government, academic, and law enforcement experts in both the United States and Mexico. Poets and critics say that perhaps

"Juárez has become a metaphor, an emblem of the future of the U.S.-Mexico border."[9] But Juárez is not a metaphor. It is a real place of great neglect and great suffering. It is a place where gangs of killers—organized and otherwise—commit murder with no fear of punishment. It is a place where the citizens can expect no protection from their government leaders or from their institutions.

On April 13, 2010, a confidential report compiled by the security ministers of the Mexican government was presented to the Mexican Senate and leaked to the Associated Press. The report said that nearly twenty-three thousand people had been killed across Mexico since December 2006 when President Calderón deployed the army in his bid to do away with drug cartels. This added more than four thousand dead to the previously published estimates in the national and international press. In mid-July, the government's official estimate was 25,500 and still climbing. A few weeks later, on August 3, 2010, the head of the Center for Investigation and National Security (CISEN) announced at a meeting hosted by President Calderón that the war against organized crime had actually killed more than twenty-eight thousand people.[10] Juárez is ground zero in this war: more than one fourth of the more than 28,000 dead that the Mexican government admits to since December 2006 (as of September 2010) have occurred in this one border city of slightly over one million people—more than 6,560 as of September 14, 2010.

I am often asked why I am keeping a daily tally to report the murders in Ciudad Juárez, and what I hope to accomplish with the Frontera-List.[11] I get many inquiries from journalists and academic researchers who tell me how difficult it is to get reliable numbers from the government offices that have the responsibility for reporting them. I think about the statement at the NAHJ panel earlier this summer where two hundred of the dead disappeared from the accounting in the space of a minute. I spend hours online trying to find accounts of violent incidents that can be used to document cases for political asylum, and I realize that the documentation of what happened could disappear from the public record forever, or it may never have been reported at all due to the ever-present and growing danger faced by Mexican journalists who can be killed for doing their jobs.

As I was revising this paper today, a friend who is a Mexican reporter seeking political asylum in the United States came to my office. He said that he had heard from friends in his hometown in northwestern Chihuahua that there had been twenty killings in the last few days in a town of about ten thousand people and that many dead bodies had been left on the town plaza. Not a single notice had appeared in the newspaper or on local TV news. This reporter covered events in several small towns in this region of Chihuahua until June 2008 when he fled to the United States after receiving a direct threat from the Mexican Army for reporting soldiers' involvement in criminal activity. He has not been replaced. Mexico is now one of the most dangerous countries in the world for journalists.[12]

I also look at the record that is available and see how certain facts and deaths can become more important than others and obscure the harsher but more ordinary reality. The case of the Juárez "femicides" is a good one to consider. During the years that the killings of women began to be noticed outside of the city in the 1990s and beyond, nearly ten times as many men as women were murdered in Juárez. The killings of these men were treated with the same impunity as the killings of women. Those in the press and academia who have written extensively about the murders of women, those who coined the term "femicide" to define the killing of women as a product of their gender, seldom acknowledge the actual numbers of victims of violence in Juárez and the fact that the killings of women are a small percentage of the total. Perhaps the focus on the murders of women enables people to feel that the situation in Juárez is containable, that it is a crime drama to be solved with good police work, with activism, consciousness-raising, protests, and a variety of artistic productions (novels, movies, art exhibitions, etc.). It seems more manageable perhaps to deal with a phenomenon in which all the victims are so obviously innocent and sympathetic. It is much more difficult and challenging to look at the huge cauldron of social pathology that Juárez has become—that Juárez has been becoming for a long time.

The products of some artists, film producers, and fiction writers about the Juárez femicides have often hijacked the sincere efforts of victims' relatives and activists in the border region and turned real stories into sensational accounts. Sex and violence always sell. The focus on gender-based homicides (femicides) has obscured the terrible reality of generalized violence in Juárez and its multiple causes that cannot be resolved nor explained by sensational theories. This is the thesis of a pioneering study by Yale researcher Erin Frey, who did in-depth research in Juárez, interviewing activists, journalists, and academics. She also analyzed statistics from government and academic sources and compiled a comprehensive bibliography of published sources about the Juárez femicides.[13]

The murders of women began to be noticed and written about in Juárez in the early 1990s and in the U.S. press a few years later. For about fifteen years, women made up about 10 to 12 percent of murder victims in the city. When the murder numbers exploded in 2008, the percentage of female victims dropped to about 5 percent while the actual numbers of all people killed increased by more than five times, and those numbers of both male and female victims continue to increase. The death toll in Juárez, as of mid-September 2010, was more than 2,180 and about 210 of those victims were women. The percentage of female victims is climbing again and this is attributed to the fact that increasing numbers of women are working in the drug business and so face the same risks as men involved in these criminal activities.

Based on the available information from police and newspaper reports, most of the women are killed in the same circumstances as the men—shot to death on the street or in their homes or in other public places like bars and shopping malls. Many women are also victimized by spouses or other male relatives or acquaintances, and in fact, during the years when the Juárez femicides became the dominant focus of activists and academics outside of Mexico, it is estimated that at least three-fourths of those cases were domestic violence.

However, much of the scholarship and activism surrounding the femicides in Juárez has focused so exclusively on the women that it has obscured the knowledge of the fate of many other victims. Since January 2008, my research has focused on documenting through media sources the unprecedented wave of violence that has engulfed the city of Juárez. When I have the opportunity to speak or write about the more than sixty-five hundred people murdered in Juárez since 2008, a common question is often: "What about the femicides?" I then explain that the number of women victimized since 1993 has ranged from a high of 18 percent to a low of 5 percent of the total, and that women account for about 9 percent of all the murder victims from 1993 to the present. From 1993 through September 10, 2010, about 878 women were murdered in Juárez and more than 9,000 men. It does not mean that the smaller percentage of female victims do not matter, but rather that *all* of the lives—of women, men, boys, and girls—matter. In the current explosion of crime and violence, all of the people of Juárez are victims, not only the women. What is happening in Juárez is much more than femicide. It is a human rights disaster.

The Frontera-List is a way to raise awareness of the day-to-day reality of the violence in Juárez. When you learn even the most basic details of the murder victims, it makes it much more difficult to believe the rhetoric of both Mexican and U.S. government officials when they say that 90 percent of the victims are criminals being killed by other criminals. President Calderón has said this explicitly and it has been echoed by his security officials, by both the U.S. and Mexican ambassadors, and by various members of the U.S. administration, including Secretary of State Hillary Clinton.

I also use the list as a *proto-archive,* a place to store thousands of original articles that document this time period in Juárez and in other places in Mexico and the border region. I am working on a plan to develop these archived articles into something that will be a real database that will allow us to find out more about the characteristics of the victims (ages, genders, circumstances of the murders, etc.). This information will be an important piece of the record of what happened.[14]

NOTES

1. "Felipe Calderón: The Man Who Took on the Drug Cartels," *Globe and Mail,* May 28, 2010, http://www.theglobeandmail.com/news/world/felipe-Calderón-the-man-who-took-on-the-drug-cartels/article1585334/.

2. The Situation Room, "Interview with Mexican President Felipe Calderón: Analysis of Special Election Results," aired May 19, 2010, http://transcripts.cnn.com/TRANSCRIPTS/1005/19/sitroom.01.html.

3. Sandra Rodríguez, "Cimbra la reunión madre de masacrados," *El Diario de Juárez,* February 12, 2010, http://www.diario.com.mx/nota.php?notaid=666f01ffcc609f1d0e8a415b99eb230d. Translation by the author.

4. "Réplicas de Villas de Salvárcar," *Lapolaka,* March 11, 2010, http://lapolaka.com/2010/03/11/replicas-de-villas-de-salvarcar/.

5. "Videogames para los *lepes,* ejecutan ladrón de puertas…," *Lapolaka,* March 12, 2010, http://lapolaka.com/2010/03/12/videogames-para-chavillos/.

6. "En medio del Infierno, Dios es grande…!" *Lapolaka,* March 13, 2010, http://lapolaka.com/2010/03/13/enmedio-del-infierno-dios-es-grande/print/. Translation by the author.

7. Molly Molloy, "Massacre at CIAD #8 in Juárez," *Narco News Bulletin,* August 18, 2008, http://www.narconews.com/Issue54/article3181.html.

8. "Fleeing Drug Violence, Mexicans Pour into the United States," *New York Times,* April 17, 2010.

9. "Juárez Is Dying, Prominent Journalist Warns," *El Paso Times,* April 10, 2010.

10. "Van 28 mil muertos por guerra a narco: Cisen," *El Universal,* August 3, 2010, http://www.diario.com.mx/nota.php?notaid=a3c6dbe8f284fa59575767ea6ce4f079.

11. http://groups.google.com/group/frontera-list.

12. "Two More Journalists Shot Dead in Continuing Media Bloodshed," *Reporters without Borders,* July 12, 2010, http://en.rsf.org/mexico-two-more-journalists-shot-dead-in-12-07-2010, 37925.html.

13. Erin Frey, "Femicide in Juárez, Mexico: The Hidden Transcript that No One Wants to Read" (unpublished honors thesis, Yale University, Branford College, Department of History, 2008). A revised version of the thesis will be submitted for publication.

14. As of the end of August 2012, about eleven thousand people have been victims of homicide in Ciudad Juarez, Mexico—an average of 6.5 murders per day since January 2008. Though the murder rate seems to be decreasing in Juarez in 2012, the violence continues to rage across Mexico. Official data releases from government agencies and media reports produce estimates of the national homicide death toll for President Calderon's sexenio (December 2006–December 2012) ranging from one hundred to one hundred fifty thousand victims.

5. Reading Leonés in New Haven: Cataloging Backlogged Materials in "Other Iberian Languages"

Ellen Jaramillo

This is a brief description of a new two-year grant-funded project that is being undertaken at Yale University Library to catalog and process approximately three thousand titles from our backlogs, which were published in Spain and Portugal but are not in the Spanish or Portuguese languages. The majority of these materials are in Catalan, Galician (also known as Gallegan), Bable (a.k.a. Asturian), Aragonese, Basque, and a number of dialects. How do we identify, locate, begin to organize, and proceed to process this material? What level of bibliographic record will need to be created? Will authority work be created?

Although it is not "Latin American" (unless you count the greater Iberian diaspora throughout Latin America), many SALALM members' duties, especially during these times of diminishing staff, have come to include responsibility for peninsular materials and studies. In light of many institutions' budget-driven mandates to reduce or to cease collecting in areas not taught in their permanent curriculum, this kind of non-mainstream library collection may well cease to grow or even to exist in future years, and this may be one of the last specific cataloging projects of its kind for the foreseeable future.

A Description of the Arcadia Grant

In February 2009, Yale University Libraries received a $5 million gift from Arcadia, a charitable foundation based in the United Kingdom. Established in 2001, Arcadia has committed more than $181 million in funding to works that protect endangered treasures of culture and nature. These include international projects to digitize endangered languages, archives, and artifacts, as well as the protection of ecosystems and environments threatened with extinction. Arcadia seeks to ensure that the scholarly resources created are widely available. This gift allows Yale to make the library's collections of international materials more available through cataloging and digitization. The gift will be paid out over five years, from 2009 to 2013, in million-dollar installments. A portion of the first payment of $1 million is helping Yale to continue its work on cataloging African language materials. With a collection that approaches thirteen million volumes, Yale University Library has long recognized its

39

responsibility for maintaining and preserving access to the wealth of resources it has acquired during the past three hundred-plus years. One of the library's Catalog and Metadata Services Department's ongoing goals is the mission of "Unlocking Hidden Collections" of lesser-known or difficult-to-obtain materials.

As in many other libraries, Yale's Catalog and Metadata Services Department has seen its staffing levels drop precipitously during this recent decade. For years now, departing staff are not being replaced. However, in a cataloging operation that supports both print and digital programs, we strive to continue to build on the strengths of our remaining staff and take advantage of their deep language, subject, and technical expertise. These are skills that are necessary to fully describe, organize, and provide intellectual access to materials that are often unique or are held in only a few collections.

With that thought in mind, along with a desire to garner some of the Arcadia funding for use in our department and the intention to further reduce our backlog of as-yet-uncataloged materials, our department head, Joan Swanekamp, had a computer query run that extracted the numbers of titles in our backlogs, sorted by language of publication. This is determined by culling the preliminary or provisional bibliographic records of items in the backlog, and sorting by the MARC (MAchine Readable Cataloging) codes for language. The department head compared the list of languages against what she knew to be the linguistic abilities of the original cataloging staff, particularly looking for pockets of lesser-known languages that would be attractive to a request to be granted some of Yale's Arcadia funding. She noted over three thousand titles published in Spain and Portugal, but which are *not* in either Spanish or Portuguese. The majority of these materials are in Catalan, followed by Galician (a.k.a. Gallegan), Bable (Asturian), Aragonese, Basque, and a number of dialects (Navarrese-Aragonese, Montañés or Cantabrian, Leonese, Extremeño, Andalusian, etc.). She asked whether I would be able to catalog them. I understand a fair amount of them in writing, except for Basque. I was hoping they would not find any Ladino, which is similar to Spanish but written in Hebrew characters; Aljamia, which is similar to Portuguese written in Arabic characters; or Gitano, because I do not know any of the Romany languages.

The department head's next step was to apply to the head university librarian for some of the Arcadia funds, in order to hire a librarian to "backfill" my position as Spanish and Portuguese language cataloger during the time I would be detailed to catalog the "other Iberian" materials. Funding was granted to fill a two-year term position, and we hired a catalog librarian with a good knowledge of Spanish, who was already working at Yale but whose term position was soon to end.

Identifying and Locating the Materials

Once we knew there were over three thousand uncataloged titles in what we have come to call "other Iberian languages," the question was how to retrieve them from the backlogs. Yale library's general backlog alone numbers around 150,000 volumes, or, roughly as much as a small college library, and it is located in several areas within the main library building. Each volume or piece is tagged with a barcode that allows the item to be tracked through the various stages of processing and, finally, circulation. An SQL (Structured Query Language) formula was written and run, asking for a list of all items in our backlogs with the following MARC language codes:

ARG (Aragonese)

AST (Bable or Asturian)

BAQ (Basque)

CAT (Catalan)

GLG (Galician or Gallegan)

We took into account the possibility that the MARC language code in the provisional or preliminary bibliographic records could be incorrectly tagged or left blank. We could not think of a mechanical way to separate these kinds of records, so we hope that during the course of the two-year project, they will be identified through human intervention as they are retrieved from the backlogs and pass through the periodic searching workflow.

The report listing the three thousand titles was given to the person over-seeing student workers, so that the students could begin to pull the items from the various backlogs for me to catalog. This list can be manipulated and sorted by language, title and author, our local database's bibliographic ID number, location and the date tracked, and barcode number. Staff members were also alerted to give me any backlogged or recently received items in these languages that they might come across. We have experienced the occasional human error, such as a book whose title and text was in French, the MARC language code was correctly tagged as French, but the author's name, Ignacio Catalan, caused some confusion!

Project Housekeeping: Tracking and Workflows

Once I had gathered a few other Iberian items, I requested some shelv-ing be set aside and requested a separate patron status to which these items could be charged, so that we could isolate them from the regular workflows and keep track of their location within the processing function. I created a detailed Excel spreadsheet to record cataloging statistics by month, separating the numbers of both titles and pieces by language or dialect and also by format (monographs, serials, DVDs, CD-ROMs, etc.). Both tasks allowed me to keep track of how much of the project had been accomplished and also to provide periodic updates to my department head, the head of the library, and to the organization funding the project.

Many of the other Iberian language items have been in Yale library's backlog since the 1970s or 1980s, so the department head made the decision that, once cataloged, they would be sent to Yale's off-campus shelving facility, rather than housed in our main library, since there has not been a high demand for them. Items housed in the shelving facility can be retrieved within twenty-four hours.

Cataloging Decisions

The vast majority of the titles cataloged so far have been single-volume monographs. There have been several serials and a few items in other formats such as CD-ROMs and DVDs. Bibliographic records are produced at either the full level or at PCC (Program for Cooperative Cataloging) core level. Library of Congress subject headings and full LC call numbers are assigned.

I am creating authority records through NACO (the name authority component of the Program for Cooperative Cataloging), in accordance with national standards and Yale's local policy. Most often this involves authority records for persons with compound surnames. A few series authority records have been created. The bibliographic records are being exported to OCLC (Online Computer Library Center) for use in cataloging by other libraries and to allow intellectual access to Yale's collections. Our department head has decided that all of the bibliographic records within this project should have a Language Note variable field (a 546, even when the language was noted in the General Description or Fixed Field). This would allow for identification of the dialects, for many of which there are no MARC language codes. The language name itself can be searched by keyword, allowing us to identify items cataloged through this project.

I have been qualifying the country of publication in the imprint field (260, delimiter "a"), and supplying a translation into Spanish for the locations when the place names in the vernacular are not well-known. For example, the place name Uviéu, appearing as the place of publication on an item would be transcribed as 260 \a Uviéu [i.e., Oviedo, Spain]. Other examples include the following:

Lleida [i.e., Lérida, Spain]

Alcoi [i.e., Alcoy, Spain]

Arboç [i.e., Arbós, Spain]

Ourense [i.e., Orense, Spain]

Gasteiz [i.e., Vitoria, Spain]

Donostia [i.e., San Sebastián, Spain]

A Coruña [i.e., La Coruña, Spain]

Iruña or Iruñea [i.e., Pamplona, Spain]

Bizkaia [i.e., Vizcaya, Spain]

Eivissa [i.e., Ibiza, Spain]

Xixón [i.e., Gijón, Spain]

Vic [i.e., Vich, Spain]

While this may be considered to be unnecessary, or even "boutique" cataloging treatment, I think it provides a service in helping to better identify the item in hand. Additionally, it is useful if there is future need to replace the item.

The Basque Question: Cataloging What You Cannot Read

Even though spoken and published in the Iberian Peninsula, Basque does not have any known linguistic relatives. It is a pre-Indo-European language geographically surrounded by Romance languages. Basque language library materials were included in the project due to geographic proximity. As with most SALALM members, I know Spanish and Portuguese, but not Basque. I found myself having to ponder the question: *how does one catalog what one cannot understand?*

My initial response to the question is "very slowly." It is easy for our unaccustomed eyes to overlook and misread or mistype the unfamiliar combinations of vowels and consonants found in Basque. The second part of the response is: look for a "hook," anything that looks familiar or that can serve as a key into the Basque text. Fortunately, a few of the items that I have cataloged were bilingual Spanish/Basque editions or had summaries or blurbs in Spanish. This helps immeasurably. Lacking those, I search the item looking for recognizable cognates.

Besides searching in OCLC (where so far I have found very little useable copy), I also try searching Basque titles, authors, or series in the online catalog of the Basque Library at the University of Nevada in Reno. There I have been able to find some brief records for some of the fiction titles and rarely have found another edition of a title that I could use as a basis for original cataloging for Yale's holdings. Finally, I look up keywords in titles or tables of content, in either a hard copy or an online dictionary. This can be somewhat tedious, but not impossible. At times this has given me the satisfaction of solving a puzzle. I have also learned that Google Translate can be somewhat helpful, even though significant amounts of imagination must be used to come up with accurate parallels.

It seems that, for the most part, Yale Library owns titles that are not in the Basque Library in Reno, so in exporting the bibliographic records that are cataloged during this project to OCLC, we are providing a service to the broader library community that will be able to use these records for their own not-yet-cataloged holdings or to request them through interlibrary loan. Therefore, I would like to suggest that in about two years' time, my cataloger colleagues might want to research in OCLC any Basque materials that they may have sitting in their backlogs. You may get lucky!

Just Do It: The Swoosh of Cataloging

Sometimes the easiest way to begin conceiving of and organizing a project is simply to get started and to develop it as you go. That is certainly the cataloger's philosophy when we are faced with a large pile of unprocessed library materials. "Divide and conquer" in this particular case means to sort the materials by language (which sometimes takes a bit of time to correctly identify) and to try to do several titles within the same language at one time, in order to avoid confusion and to develop a pattern or rhythm in cataloging the materials.

Prior to beginning the project, I reviewed the LC language and literature schedules (the P class) for these languages. That did not help when I needed to classify a book of poems by a single author in Aragonese. There is a problem with where to class fiction works in underdeveloped LC schedules. The PC subclass is clearly for linguistic works, so the call number for "Texts" would not apply.

While there are LC subject headings established for several of the other languages, there are no subjects for Aragonese fiction. There is "Spanish language—Dialects—Spain—Aragon," but that subject is intended for philology, linguistics and literary studies in general, and not for a specific work of fiction. There is "Spanish language—Spain—León," but that is for the regional variation of the Spanish language spoken or written there. There is within the PQ subclass "Spanish poetry (or literature)—Spain—Aragon," but this is for general regional literature of the area.

PC4781–4784	Navarrese-Aragonese Called codialect by Leite de Vasconcellos in distinction from Portuguese dialects proper
PC 4781.A1–.A5	Periodicals. Societies. Serials. Collections (non-serial)
PC 4781.A6–Z	General works. Grammar
PC 4782	Dictionaries
PC 4783	Texts
PC 4784.A–.Z9	Local, by dialect name or place, A–Z
	For language groups use local number for works too general to be classed with an individual language or separately classed smaller group
PC 4784.A–.Z9	Translations into foreign languages. By language, A–Z. Subarrange by date.

Fig. 1. Library of Congress Class P schedule, subclass PC: PC4781–4784. *Classification Web,* http://classificationweb.net/ (accessed May 22, 2010).

Aragon

PQ7001.A7   History

PQ7001.A72   Collections

PQ7001.A73   Translations

Fig. 2. Library of Congress Class P schedule, subclass PQ: PQ7001. *Classification Web,* http://classificationweb.net/ (accessed May 22, 2010).

The solution is to class the Aragonese poet as one would a Spaniard, under "Spanish literature—Individual authors," within the appropriate time period. However, this does not take into account that the individual author may be writing in a language other than Spanish! The time constraint of this project has not afforded me time enough to propose to the Library of Congress that a few subject and class changes be made.

Lessons and Findings (So Far)

Searching over three hundred backlogged items in OCLC, in two months I have found a total of six full-level LC records for some of the items, with LC subjects and call number. Fewer than 10 percent of the items have had records created by other English-speaking institutions, many with incomplete copy or requiring authority work. Many titles have had preliminary vendor records in Spanish, such as those from Puvill Libros, or bibliographic records from the Biblioteca Nacional de España. These vernacular records require the creation of a parallel record with English language subjects and description, which will be exported to OCLC for other English-speaking libraries to use and to record Yale's holdings for interlibrary loan. Everything else so far, or about 88 percent, has needed original cataloging, which I am doing at either the "Full" or "Core" levels.

Less than two months into the project, I have fully cataloged 212 titles (225 volumes) and created thirty-five NACO authority records. Far and away the largest number of items cataloged have been in Catalan (which is good for me since I find it easiest to read), and I think it will most likely remain that way throughout the duration of the project. Galician is next, then Basque, followed by Bable (Asturian), and the others. I have not received anything in an Iberian dialect yet, but then we have not gone through the entire backlog.

As someone who had cataloged only Latin Americana for several decades, I have been finding that many of the titles are taking me longer to catalog than I am used to, certainly longer than it would take me to do a similar Latin American imprint. I attribute this to my unfamiliarity with some sections of the LC class schedules for these areas and also my unfamiliarity with the history of Catalan, Galician, and Basque literature, famous persons, and local politics. Sometimes a little additional research is required, and I am particularly enjoying this aspect of the project. I am learning a fair amount about the autonomous regions of Spain and recent politics and economic trends. I am also getting good at using *Viquipèdia* (the Catalan language "Wikipedia").

I have been mildly surprised to find that so far only about 40 percent of what I have cataloged has been *belle lettres* or fiction titles. The remaining 60 percent have been in a wide variety of subject areas, including labor relations, audiovisual use in education, dubbing and translating for films, Internet information security, maxims, handmade wooden toys, and stone crucifixes. Percentage spreads have been fairly consistent across the several languages included in the project. They are also similar to percentage spreads across subject areas that I have observed during years of cataloging Latin American materials.

El Dinosaure Català: When Budget Shortfalls Force Us to Forego Collecting Esoteric Titles

In a posthumously published article by our dear friend and colleague Scott Van Jacob, Scott writes: "Spain ranks among the top publishing countries in the world...with Barcelona alone being home to at least 278 publishers including Planeta, which is among the ten largest publishing conglomerates in the world."[1] In 1983, Spain legislated the use of its regional languages as the primary language of education within those regions, ensuring that year after year, more and more students graduate who are proficient in both their regional language as well as Spanish. The end of Spanish censorship in all languages during the last century, along with the government's elevation of the regional languages to co-official status in tandem with Spanish, promotes a continuous increase in the numbers of people able to speak, read, and write their regional tongues. Additionally, the Spanish government provides subsidies to publishers that produce titles in the regional languages, so it is no wonder that the publishers that Scott interviewed are confident about the future of Catalan language publishing. The same benefits accrue for the other regional languages due to government support and an ever-increasing potential readership. Therefore it is not surprising, as Scott noted, that between 2002 and 2007, publications appearing in Catalan increased by 5 percent. It is good that there are more and more Spaniards proficient in Catalan who will be potential purchasers of this increasing catalog of titles, because it appears as though the market in the United States for "minority" language materials may well be drying up.

A recent internal Yale library document on collection development policy for Spanish and Portuguese languages and literatures states:

> In addition to the extensive collection of Spanish and Portuguese literature, the Sterling Library houses a rich array of resources related to the Basque Language and Romance languages in the Iberian Peninsula, including reference works, bibliographies, works on origin and history of language, lexicographical works, and comparative language studies. The collection includes

all languages and literatures of the Iberian Peninsula, including Basque, Catalán-Valencian-Balearic, Galician (Gallegan), and even Bable, Occitan and Leonese.[2]

Two days after this was written, a Town Hall meeting for Yale library selectors was held, at which our interim university librarian "explained that one of the ways in which the Library will comply with the budget reductions mandated by the University is by taking an additional $3 million from the Central Library collections funds. This is to be implemented strategically rather than across the board."[3] He further went on to state:

> if the measures undertaken so far by the University achieve the intended results—we will face a flat budget for the next two to three years, followed by slow endowment growth. However, we have to keep in mind that the general economy will recover at a faster pace than the endowments of large academic institutions. Therefore, we have to think in the long term—five years or more—and accept the fact that we are experiencing a major shift in collection development expectations.[4]

The interim university librarian presented a list of "Formats and Types of Materials to Be Eliminated or Reduced," which was drafted in order to provide tangible guidelines for budget proposals that target certain areas rather than impose an across-the-board reduction. Two of those categories of materials whose acquisition will be eliminated or reduced are

> very low use materials that would go to LSF [the off-campus Library Shelving Facility] because of infrequent consultation [and] Materials that can't readily be processed—[due to] quantity, language, formats. More than before, selectors should think twice (and consult with each other, as well as with other departments potentially involved, such as Cataloging or Preservation) before purchasing materials that require a lot of work because of their complexity, processing, or preservation needs.[5]

Since the materials covered in this "other Iberian languages" project are destined to be shelved off-campus, and because they require a lot of work due to language and scarcity of useable copy cataloging done by other institutions, these are exactly the kinds of materials whose acquisition will be targeted to be eliminated or reduced.

In response to a question from an area studies curator about whether selectors should consult with faculty members in regard to reducing materials in their specific areas, the interim university librarian was quoted in the minutes as having replied: "The Library is going to collect materials in new areas of curricular growth related to permanent faculty positions; it is not going to support scholarly programs or research interests tied to temporary positions. The question we should ask academic departments is: Do you anticipate new permanent positions that will require the Library to collect materials in specific areas?"[6]

Yale does not offer classes in Catalan, Galician (Gallegan), Bable, Basque, or any other languages of the Iberian Peninsula except for Spanish and Portuguese. Therefore, in order to deal with a diminishing annual budget for new library materials, while trying to support new areas of curricular and research growth, Yale will be buying far fewer, if any, materials in these other Iberian languages. I imagine that Yale is not the only institution employing this strategy in trying to cope with a rapidly dwindling acquisitions budget. This situation raises some questions.

Do major research libraries like Yale risk compromising our mission when budget shortfalls force us to forego collecting esoteric titles or to stop collecting in areas where the current curriculum does not offer any classes? What will the consequences be when university libraries no longer purchase the very things that make our individual collections unique?

In the article entitled "Rethinking Research Library Collections: A Policy Framework for Straitened Times, and Beyond," our fellow SALALM colleague Dan Hazen offered some general principles to guide academic libraries as they move towards the future. He writes: "As budgets decline and priorities shift, many academic libraries will steer their acquisitions toward the basic texts and sources required for curricular support. These holdings will be heavily redundant across different institutions. Conversely, more and more noncore materials may be entirely missed."[7] How do we then, as collectors and organizers of the global cultural record, address "missing" those kinds of materials? How much does it matter, to my university and to others, that we may no longer be purchasing anything by or about Galician linguist, journalist, and historian Manuel Murguía (who was the husband of the romantic movement poetess Rosalía de Castro), or building a small collection on a timely subject like the social and educational problems assimilating recent immigrants to Spain within the regional culture of Catalonia?

Hazen suggests that "cooperative activities will become increasingly central to library programs and strategies."[8] Libraries have been engaged in cooperative activity for decades, but these recent economic times are the worst that I can recall in the past thirty-five years. We are trying to manage with the twin curse of diminishing library budgets for both staff and acquisitions, while dealing with a graying profession, especially within the area studies collections. Could there be some other strategy that we can investigate? I do not know enough about acquisitions work to begin to suggest solutions for our collections. Catalogers organize and provide intellectual and physical access to whatever items selectors purchase. But this leaves me wondering, will I be the last librarian to read Leonese in New Haven? More importantly, will I be the last to read and organize Leonese and its fellow Iberian languages if major research libraries are no longer able to purchase these materials?

NOTES

1. Scott Van Jacob and Robin Vose, "A Report on Catalan Language Publishing," *Publishing Research Quarterly* 26, no. 2 (June 2010): 129–43.

2. Lidia Uziel, "Collection Development Policy for Spanish and Portuguese Languages and Literatures at Yale" (internal Yale University Library document, March 13, 2010).

3. Minutes, Yale University Library Selectors' Town Hall Meeting, March 15, 2010.

4. Ibid.

5. Ibid.

6. Ibid.

7. Dan Hazen, "Rethinking Research Library Collections: A Policy Framework for Straitened Times, and Beyond," *Library Resources and Technical Services* 54, no. 2 (April 2010): 115–21.

8. Ibid.

6. From Trash to Treasure: Incorporating the Voices of the Marginalized into the Collection of Indiana University Libraries

C. Denise Stuempfle

Within recent years, Indiana University's Herman B Wells Library in Bloomington has acquired a large collection of *libros cartoneros* from Latin America. Information about these publications came not by means of a traditional publisher's catalog, but by word of mouth. Luis González, Indiana University Libraries' Latin American bibliographer, was alerted to their existence by a colleague at the University of Wisconsin–Madison and actively sought their acquisition. He eventually succeeded in amassing representative samples from Argentina, Brazil, Chile, Mexico, Paraguay, Peru, and Uruguay. To date, approximately one hundred of these books have been cataloged and await final processing. Although they come to us from several different locales, the libros cartoneros share an unusual and fascinating history, which is revealed in each book produced. Considered *libros objetos* (collectors' items) by some, artists' books by others, the unique nature of these books demands an equally unique approach to their treatment, particularly with respect to their descriptive cataloging, authority work, and eventual location within the library's collection.

Economist Gustavo A. Del Angel observes that "societies faced with economic hardship manage to find answers and create rules for a game in which the final outcome may come as a surprise."[1] So it is with the libros cartoneros. Born out of the economic crisis of 2001 in Argentina, they continue to be a symbol of sociopolitical struggle in the Latin American region. My objective in this paper is to highlight some of the issues surrounding the publication of these literary works and the challenges of processing them on the Bloomington campus of the Indiana University Libraries.

What Are the Libros Cartoneros?

Let me start with a few short definitions:

- *cartón:* cardboard

- *cartonero:* an individual who collects recyclable materials

- *libro cartonero:* a type of chapbook

- *cartonera:* a small alternative press

Manufactured by cartoneras, libros cartoneros are chapbooks whose texts are generally photocopied and whose covers are made of recycled cardboard decorated with unique hand-painted designs. Each book, therefore, is singular in its appearance. It is one-of-a-kind. Although book covers may have varying degrees of decoration, there is generally no attempt to disguise the corrugated cardboard from which they are made. Cover design is entirely the choice of the creator who may be a full-time worker or associate of the cartonera, a visitor, or a child belonging to the community. In fact, book cover design is often done by the children of cartoneros. However, policies concerning this responsibility vary among cartoneras.

The text of each book is attached to the cardboard cover with glue, wire, or thread. Limited editions of a work may include 50 to 150 copies. By agreement, authors receive no royalties but retain the rights to their works. Copies are sold at cost price. Though libros cartoneros were first created in Buenos Aires in 2003, they have since been produced in many other parts of Latin America.

Fig. 1. Two different covers of the title *Duas palavras,* published by Dulcinéia Catadora in São Paulo, Brazil. Photographs courtesy of Dulcinéia Catadora.[2]

Authorship and Content

Authors of libros cartoneros come from various backgrounds; some are academics, some are cartoneros, some are well-known writers. However, many are contemporary, first-time, or emerging authors, some of whom have been deemed "impublicables" and "los marginados."[3] This wide range of authors is in keeping with the mission of cartoneras, which is to democratize literature, to make Latin American works widely accessible, and to nurture a love for reading. Some authors publish under their real names, others use pseudonyms; some are deceased, while others inhabit the world of YouTube and the blogosphere.

In terms of their content, the libros cartoneros represent all literary genres, perhaps with a bias towards poetry. Many of the works are original, some are selections of previously published works by established authors, and others are translations. Popular themes include politics, human rights, and the arts—particularly the visual arts and their place in contemporary society.

Cartoneras and Cartoneros

The term "cartonera" originated in Buenos Aires and its origin is credited to the pioneer publishing collective Eloísa Cartonera, for whom it has special significance. Derived from "cartonero" (urban recycler), it is meant as a salute to the cartoneros of Buenos Aires for the resilience and creativity that they displayed during the economic crisis experienced by Argentina during the period 1998–2003. As the cartonera movement spread throughout Latin America, however, the term appears to have lost its original meaning and a more literal interpretation seems to have been adopted elsewhere. The association between cartón and cartonera is, of course, an easy one to make, since cartón is the primary material used by these publishing houses. In any event, the cartoneros typically supply the cartoneras with the recycled cardboard needed for their

Fig. 2. Office of the publishing collective Eloísa Cartonera, established in Buenos Aires, Argentina, in 2003. Photograph courtesy of Eloísa Cartonera.

Fig. 3. Cartoneros at work in Buenos Aires, Argentina. Photograph courtesy of Clarín.com.

book covers, for which the cartoneras are willing to pay significantly more than the cartoneros would receive from recycling companies. In addition, some cartoneros contribute to the creative aspect of the book manufacturing process as authors or artists.

Cataloging the Libros Cartoneros

For the most part, the libros cartoneros have traditional features that facilitate descriptive cataloging: author-title information, title page, imprint information, and numbered pages. Some even include biographical sketches of authors, for which any cataloger is eternally grateful! With respect to ISBNs, these are absent from earlier works but are increasingly apparent in later publications by cartoneras, such as Animita Cartonera.

In order to capture some of the richness of detail associated with these works, the Herman B Wells Library uses the Note area (500), the Subject Heading (650), and Genre Heading (655) fields consistently in bibliographical records of all libros cartoneros.

Although the libros cartoneros cannot justifiably be categorized as artists' books, art is a key aspect of their identity, as manifested by their colorful cardboard covers which serve as a distinguishing feature. Indiana University Libraries, therefore, considers it important to document this aspect of the process in each record.

If a description of the manufacturing process is contained within the book itself, it is used either in its entirety or in part as a quoted note, and the source is cited. (Most of these statements appear within the preliminary pages of the book.) Otherwise, the library uses its own version of a description. For example, Dulcinéia Catadora typically includes the following note on the leaf preceding the title page of its publications: "Capa pintada à mão por artistas e filhos de catadores, feita com papelão comprador de cooperativas de materiais recicláveis." In the absence of such a note on the item, Indiana University

Libraries would use "Recycled corrugated paperboard binding with unique hand-painted acrylic paint embellishment by members of…"

Additional Access Points

Publishing houses rarely appear as added entries in bibliographical records, since imprint information has been allocated a place in the 260 MARC 21 field. However, the Wells Library has elected to make an exception to this practice with respect to the libros cartoneros. The justification for this lies in the descriptions of these publishing houses, which emphasize the importance of the multiple roles that they play. Moreover, they are the motivators, or as the cartonera Yerba Mala asserts, the instigators behind these works. The following are excerpts from two of their manifestos: "YiYi Jambo es un proyecto artístico-editorial que nace en Asunción…. Los objetivos, entre otros, son la democratización del libro, la lectura, la creación literaria y artística originales";[4] and "Eloísa Cartonera es un proyecto artístico, social y comunitario sin fines de lucro…donde cartoneros cruzan ideas con artistas y escritores."[5]

It is clear from these descriptions that these publishing houses have a common purpose—that of improving the quality of life of their communities through the promotion of reading, art, and other cultural activities.

Establishing Authority Records

Once the decision was taken to create additional access points for the cartoneras, the next step was to establish an authority record for each cartonera. This was not without its challenges. In 2009, Johana Kunin noted: "Six years. Ten countries. Twenty initiatives with the same 'surname' (or what the market research specialists would call 'brand name' or even 'branding').… I am referring to the spread of the Latin American 'cardboard publishers,' a social initiative that is promoted mainly by independent writers and artists from the region."[6] With the growth of this movement, the prospect of establishing name headings for over twenty corporate bodies, all sharing the same last name, would seem a daunting task for any cataloger. However, this turned out not to be quite the case. As more libros cartoneros made their way to my desk, cartoneras with unique names (for example, YiYi Jambo/Yambo, Katarina Kartonera, Mburukujarami Kartonera, and Yerba Mala) were interspersed among them and the task seemed less challenging.

In all cases of cartoneras that share the last name "Cartonera," it was clear that the "name-as-presented" was intended to include "Cartonera" and that this word was not being used generically. Carl Horne, Indiana University Libraries' liaison for the Name Authority Cooperative (NACO) Program, has observed that "both the format of presentation and the exact wording of a corporate body's name strongly affect the choices we make in formulating its heading."[7] Thus, in spite of the fact that "Cartonera" served as a common last name for many of these publishers, it would have to be used. Moreover, it would have

```
010      no2010045914
040      InU ‡b eng ‡c InU
110 2    Propia Cartonera (Nuevo París, Uruguay)
410 2    Editorial La Propia Cartonera (Nuevo París, Uruguay)
410 2    Propia (Firm: Nuevo París, Uruguay)
670      Mil gotas, 2009: ‡b t.p. (La Propia Cartonera) leaf preceding t.p.
         (Editorial La Propia Cartonera, Nuevo París, Uruguay)
670      La Propia Cartonera WWW page, viewed Feb. 26, 2010:
         ‡b (La Propia)
670      La Diaria, WWW page, viewed March 1, 2010: ‡b (La Propia;
         first cartonera in Uruguay; est. 2009)
```

Fig. 4. Name Authority Record for La Propia Cartonera (excerpt).

```
010      no2010045915
040      InU ‡b eng ‡c InU
151      Nuevo París (Uruguay)
451      Balneario Nuevo París (Uruguay)
670      Sachet, 2009 ‡b leaf preceding t.p. (Nuevo París, Uruguay)
670      GEOnet, March 17, 2010 ‡b (Nuevo París; ppl; 34°51'S,
         056°14'W; variant: Balneario Nuevo París)
781 0    ‡z Uruguay ‡z Nuevo París
```

Fig. 5. Geographic Authority Record for Nuevo París, location of La Propia Cartonera (excerpt).

to be considered part of the name heading since it appeared in the chief source of information (the title page, in most instances). Often the name is presented differently on the leaf opposite the title page or on the website of the respective cartonera. Here, the name generally includes the more traditional "Editorial," "Ediciones," or "Ediçoes." These different presentations serve as variants and are documented in the 410 area of the authority record. The name authority record for La Propia Cartonera provides a good example of this.

Formulating the Name Heading for La Cartonera

The establishment of an authority record for La Cartonera of Cuernavaca, Mexico, posed some special challenges since this cartonera lacked a unique name. In formulating name headings, articles are considered routine omissions from the "name-as-presented." Thus, we were left with "Cartonera," which has already been identified as common to many publishers of libros cartoneros. The choice of "Cartonera" as a name heading for this cartonera would, therefore, not have been useful. In accordance with Anglo-American Cataloguing Rules guidelines, we decided that the use of a descriptive term would help to convey the idea that this was a corporate body (AACRII, 24.4B). In such circumstances, the addition of "Firm," "Organization," or "Project" would lend

```
010     no2010045909
040     InU ǂb eng ǂc InU
110 2   Cartonera (Firm: Cuernavaca (Mexico))
410 2   Ediciones La Cartonera (Cuernavaca (Mexico))
670     Marilyn Monroe, comunista, 2009: ǂb t.p. (La Cartonera;
        Cuernavaca, Morelos (Mexico) p. 3 of cover
        (edicioneslacartonera)
670     Akademia cartonera, 2009: ǂb p. 178 (La Cartonera;
        est. Feb., 2008, in Cuernavaca)
```

Fig. 6. Name Authority Record for La Cartonera of Cuernavaca, Mexico (excerpt).

distinction to the authorized name, which is, of course, the main purpose of an authority record.

Descriptions of these publishing houses as cooperatives, antiestablishment associations, artistic projects, literary movements, nonprofit editorial projects, or community spaces where children of cartoneros could engage with books and authors (while expanding their horizons and building their self-esteem) offer insights into their hybrid nature and tell us what cartoneras do, apart from publishing. References to such activities appear in different areas of the libros cartoneros and as slogans on website home pages. For example, "Katarina Kartonera é um projeto editorial de caráter literário, filosófico e artístico, de vanguarda, com un pensamento sem fronteira, autônomo, sem vínculo oficial institucional algum."[8] However, these self-descriptions tend not to be helpful in terms of arriving at a descriptive term that would contribute towards the creation of a distinctive name heading for each cartonera. Since cartoneras are publishing houses and use ".com" in their website addresses, we decided to use "Firm" whenever a descriptive term is needed for clarification.

Series

Series are another important collocation device for book collections. As nontraditional as these books often are, there are some that are organized as series. Series entries provide yet another form of access to these materials. In all cases, authority records are prepared and contributed to OCLC. Some of these series have unique titles, such as Yi-Yi Jambo's "Colección de poesía y narrativa sudaka-transfronteriza 'Abran Karajo.'"

Providing Subject Access to the Libros Cartoneros

When I began to work on this project in 2009, "Chapbooks, Brazilian" and "Chapbooks, Chilean" were the only subject headings to denote chapbooks emanating from the Latin American region. Gradually, I have attempted to fill this gap by submitting proposals for new subject headings to the Library of Congress. The Library of Congress Subject Headings (LCSH) list now includes "Chapbooks, Argentine" and "Chapbooks, Peruvian," while approval is pending on "Chapbooks, Mexican," "Chapbooks, Paraguayan," and "Chapbooks, Uruguayan."

Provision of this type of collocation is particularly important when cataloging literary works, since these are not normally assigned subject headings. The addition of the form subdivision "Specimens" to these subject headings signals to the researcher that chapbooks are not the content but the format of the works (for example, "Chapbooks, Argentine—Specimens").

Genre Headings

While subject headings are designed to provide access to the content of a work, genre headings describe what a work is. They also indicate that the work belongs to a specific category and suggest access to similar material in this format. The choice of "Corrugated paperboard bindings" as a Genre heading for the libros cartoneros represents an apt description of these items. Access to the entire collection of libros cartoneros can therefore be achieved through this genre search.

Conclusion

In conclusion, the benefits of incorporating these books into the collection of Indiana University Libraries go beyond their physical appeal. In addition to their artistic value, the books' method of publication, diverse authorship, and varied subject matter provide a wealth of research opportunities for scholars across the disciplines. Our role as librarians in providing access and drawing attention to these works, especially via our contributions to the Library of Congress master files, ensures that the libros cartoneros will be a subject of research for years to come. Moreover, our cooperative efforts in acquiring and cataloging this new form of publication will enable some of the voices of the marginalized in Latin America to be heard.

NOTES

1. Gustavo A. Del Angel, review of *The Decline of Latin American Economies: Growth, Institutions, and Crises,* ed. Sebastian Edwards, Gerardo Esquivel, and Graciela Márquez, *Business History Review* 82, no. 3 (Fall 2008).

2. This title is not in the holdings of Indiana University Libraries. It is included here to illustrate the unique character of individual book covers of libros cartoneros.

3. Cecilia Durán, "Surge la nueva editorial La Rueda Cartonera," *La Jornada Jalisco*, November 13, 2009, http://www.lajornadajalisco.com.mx/2009/11/13/index.php?section=cultura&article=012n2cul.

4. Yiyi Jambo, http://yiyijambo.blogspot.com/2007/10/4.html.

5. Eloísa Cartonera, http://baspotting.blogspot.com/2006/12/elosa-cartonera.html.

6. Joana Kunin, "Notes on the Expansion of the Latin American Cardboard Publishers: Reporting Live from the Field," in *Akademia Cartonera: A Primer of Latin American Cartonera Publishers* (accompanying disc), ed. Ksenija Bilbija and Paloma Celis Carbajal (Madison: Parallel Press/University of Wisconsin–Madison Libraries, 2009), p. 31.

7. Personal communication, 2009.

8. Katarina Kartonera, http://katarinakartonera.wikidot.com/kensomos.

BIBLIOGRAPHY

Bilbija, Ksenija, and Paloma Celis Carbajal, eds. *Akademia Cartonera: A Primer of Latin American Cartonera Publishers.* Madison: Parallel Press/University of Wisconsin–Madison Libraries, 2009.

Del Angel, Gustavo A. Review of *The Decline of Latin American Economies: Growth, Institutions, and Crises,* edited by Sebastian Edwards, Gerardo Esquivel, and Graciela Marquez. *Business History Review* 82, no. 3 (Fall 2008).

Kunin, Joana. "Notes on the Expansion of the Latin American Cardboard Publishers: Reporting Live from the Field." In *Akademia Cartonera: A Primer of Latin American Cartonera Publishers* (accompanying disc), edited by Ksenija Bilbija and Paloma Celis Carbajal, 31–51. Madison: Parallel Press/University of Wisconsin–Madison Libraries, 2009.

APPENDIX

Libros Cartoneros on Exhibition during Presentation

Chávez, Juan Manuel. *Sin cobijo en Palomares.* [Lima, Peru]: Sarita Cartonera, 2004.

Drucaroff, Elsa. *Leyenda erótica.* [Buenos Aires, Argentina]: Eloísa Cartonera, 2006.

Filho, João. *Três Sibilas.* [São Paulo, Brazil]: Dulcinéia Catadora, 2008.

Navarro Honores, Jorge Luis. *Testigo.* Santiago, Chile: Ediciones Animita Cartonera, 2007.

Oda, Teruko. *Vento leste.* [Sâo Paulo, Brazil]: Dulcinéia Catadora, 2008.

Pougy, Eliana. *Poesiaminha nada.* [São Paulo, Brazil]: Dulcinéia Catadora, 2007.

Saavedra, Edgar. *Final aún.* [Lima], Peru: Sarita Cartonera, 2004.

Terron, Joca Reiners. *Uma antologia bêbada: Fábulas da mercearia.* [São Paulo, Brazil]: Dulcinéia Catadora, 2008.

7. Teaching Ancient Mesoamerica: A Collaborative Faculty/Librarian Experiment in Embedment

David C. Murray

Several years ago, librarians at Temple University won the right to develop and implement a formal Information Literacy (IL) program within the General Education (GenEd) curriculum. A committee of librarians met to build on outcomes and learning activities that had already been developed for the first-year GenEd writing course titled English 0802: Analytical Reading and Writing. Today at Temple, instructors of this course can neither opt out of the two mandatory library sessions nor change the predetermined IL outcomes. Most instructors are happy to work with librarians to meet shared IL outcomes.

Significant among the several benefits of this arrangement, certainly from the librarians' perspective, is the fact that IL outcomes are now integrated into the curriculum to an extent once thought unimaginable only ten years ago. Many English 0802 instructors are reporting (anecdotally) improvements in their students' research skills. In one important way, however, Temple librarians have become victims of their own success: it is difficult for the dozen full-time members of the Reference and Instructional Services Department to teach an average of 130 sections (or 260 distinct class periods) of English 0802 offered every fall and spring semester. Additionally, the following challenges remain to be addressed:

- Some librarians feel that the "old one-shot" has morphed into the "new two-shot." Several would like to have even more formal, structured interactions with students.

- It is not yet feasible to track student learning. Instead student "satisfaction" is elicited in a two-minute, postworkshop evaluation. Students are asked whether or not the librarian presented the information "clearly and effectively," and if the information presented was relevant to the research assignment. Students are also asked what they found most and least useful about the two workshops.

- Ultimately, the librarians continue to be reliant upon individual faculty buy-in, although to a lesser extent than before. A few faculty members simply "teach around" the library sessions.

Some of these challenges can be mitigated by moving to a greater level of classroom integration or by "embedding librarians into the classroom." In practice, academic librarians do not generally take the concept of information literacy as seriously as a reader of the information science literature might expect. If information literacy is so central to our mission as reference and instruction librarians, why—despite the well-known deficiencies of our current one-shots—do we not take greater responsibility for ensuring that our students develop IL skills? Why are measures for tracking student learning often missing from our IL instruction? Why, ultimately, have we not demanded greater responsibility for teaching in a domain within which librarians are particularly well suited? The latter question is often answered with the following:

- Information literacy is not a discipline but rather a set of skills or learning outcomes that apply across all disciplines. One cannot teach IL like history, literature, or biology. Indeed, for IL instruction to be effective, it must be grounded in the disciplines.

- I am a librarian, not a member of the teaching faculty. It is not my job and/or I do not feel qualified to teach college-level courses. Besides, my position entails too many other responsibilities.

- The faculty will do the job if we provide them guidance.

The literature does not agree on a definition for librarian embedment, but essentially an embedded librarian is one who spends time with students and faculty outside the library, for example, office hours and especially time in the classroom. The literature suggests that students will learn to find, evaluate, and use information more effectively when librarians become active and integral course participants, for example, developing and grading assignments.

Keeping the latter in mind, and hoping to counter any arguments against even greater librarian embedment, Ron Webb, Temple University's director of Latin American Studies, and I worked throughout fiscal year 2009–2010 to jointly develop a writing-intensive IL course for Latin American Studies titled LAS 2098: The Legacy of Mesoamerica. The appropriate Temple University committees, that is, the Committee on Instruction and the Writing-Intensive Course Committee, approved our course in May 2010. As of this writing, it is expected to run in fall 2011 or spring 2012. The vice provost and director of the Temple University Writing Center wrote of our course proposal: "The [Writing-Intensive Course] committee members appreciated the depth of the 'information literacy' component of this course. We have never seen a w-course proposal that presented such a thorough and interesting approach to teaching students about finding and using sources." An associate professor of Spanish stated: "We [the Committee on Instruction] were all impressed with the integration of the library component in this course. You have set a very innovative precedent for such collaboration and we expect that others in the college will follow suit."

The librarian's role in LAS 2098 will be to develop and deliver up to five class lectures, that is, disciplinary course content, that will include a special emphasis on IL outcomes; to develop and grade the annotated bibliography portion of the research paper (25 percent of grade), IL activity (10 percent of grade), and IL assignment (10 percent of grade); and to provide substantial out-of-class support in the form of a research guide and office hours. The research guide including IL assignments are available online at http://guides. temple.edu/las2098.

BIBLIOGRAPHY

Bowler, Meagan, and Kori Street. "Investigating the Efficacy of Embedment: Experiments in Information Literacy Integration." *Reference Services Review* 36, no. 4 (2008): 438–49.

Dewey, Barbara I. "The Embedded Librarian: Strategic Campus Collaborations." *Resource Sharing and Information Networks* 17, no. 1 (2004): 5–17.

Dugan, Mary. "Embedded Librarians in an Ag Econ Class: Transcending the Traditional." *Journal of Agricultural and Food Information* 9, no. 4 (2008): 301–9.

Eke, K. J. "Team Teaching with an Embedded Librarian." *Distance Education Report* 12, no. 17 (2008): 6–7.

Freiburger, Gary, and Sandra Kramer. "Embedded Librarians: One Library's Model for Decentralized Service." *Journal of the Medical Library Association* 97, no. 2 (2009): 139–42.

Hearn, Michael R. "Embedding a Librarian in the Classroom: An Intensive Information Literacy Model." *Reference Services Review* 33, no. 2 (2005): 219–27.

Julien, Heidi, and Lisa M. Given. "Faculty-Librarian Relationships in the Information Literacy Context: A Content Analysis of Librarians' Expressed Attitudes and Experiences." *Canadian Journal of Information and Library Sciences* 27, no. 3 (2002): 65–87.

Kesselman, Martin A., and Sarah B. Watstein. "Creating Opportunities: Embedded Librarians." *Journal of Library Administration* 49, no. 4 (2009): 383–400.

Owens, Rachel. "Where the Students Are: The Embedded Librarian Project at Daytona Beach College." *Florida Libraries* 51, no. 1 (2008): 8–10.

Partello, Peggie. "Librarians in the Classroom." *Reference Librarian* 43, no. 89 (2005): 107–20.

Ramsay, Karen M., and Jim Kinnie. "The Embedded Librarian." *Library Journal* 131, no. 6 (2006): 34–35.

8. Coming of Age through Digitization: The Oral History Programme at the University of the West Indies, St. Augustine, Trinidad and Tobago

Kathleen Helenese-Paul

History of the Program

The Oral and Pictorial Records Programme (OPReP) was established in 1981 at the University of the West Indies to gather historical data on Trinidad and Tobago. OPReP is the second such initiative in the English-speaking Caribbean; the Social History Project at the University of the West Indies at Mona being the first.[1] The program has three main functions: conducting and storing voice-recorded interviews with participants or witnesses in significant historical and cultural events; collecting photographs of people, events, and buildings of historical importance; and identifying other similar repositories of historical materials.

The program is currently converting the recordings from their original analog format to digital format. This process, which is taking place at the Alma Jordan Library, the University of the West Indies, St. Augustine, is the focus of this paper.[2]

Organization

When OPReP was established in 1981, it was deemed necessary to identify themes or topics that "could fill the gaps in historical knowledge."[3] Among these topics were emancipation (which was declared in 1834), Indian Arrival Day, the development of calypso and steel band, early oil exploration, general elections, and sports (cricket in particular). The next step was to identify and interview notable persons with intimate knowledge of the various topics. Among the early participants were the historians C. L. R. James and Sir Ellis Clarke.[4] Early on, special attention was paid to the St. Augustine Campus in view of the fact that it was established in 1960 when the Imperial College of Tropical Agriculture (I.C.T.A.) and the University College of the West Indies (U.C.W.I.) merged. Anyone who was involved with the establishment of the campus and who was available was interviewed including the first campus principal, the first campus librarian, and holders of the first professorial chairs.

A more recent and noteworthy effort has been the partnering with the university's Centre for Creative and Festival Arts, whereby students taking courses in steel pan history and development have contributed their interviews with members of the national steel bands, pan tuners, and arrangers.

Recordings

To date, 144 interviews have been conducted and recorded using standard cassette tapes. At the outset, these interviews were transcribed though on a limited scale due to lack of personnel and as requested by researchers. In 2001, additional personnel were hired to transcribe the backlog of interviews, and by 2003 a total of 109 interviews had been transcribed. The next step is the conversion of the transcripts to Portable Document Format (PDF) files.

Digitization for Preservation and Access

Digitizing the OPReP audio recordings and transferring the digital information to the library's managed digital repository was seen as the most feasible channel for maintaining access to this valued content over the long term. The library has recognized the fact that the audio cassette magnetic tapes on which the recordings were stored would eventually become prone to degradation, and that technical advances would soon make the analog material and its associated players/readers increasingly obsolete. In addition, more recent oral history interviews have been recorded on digital media, thus making the development of an appropriate methodology for archiving material in digital formats a requirement. The need to digitize the older OPReP recordings was largely driven by the necessity of preserving the audio material, and therefore was a priority.

A by-product of digitization is the opportunity for enhanced access, and the library was keen not just to digitize for the sake of preservation, but also to facilitate improved and more efficient access by the institution's stakeholders. The recommendation here revolved around providing a web interface for delivering streaming podcasts of the digital oral history interviews. The archival copies of the digital files would be stored on optical disks and external hard drives, while the access copies would be housed in the institutional repository that was being deployed by the library at the time.

OPReP Conversion

Deliberations on the acquisition of suitable equipment for the conversion process began in 2004 and continued into 2005 as efforts were put into sourcing a device that would link the analog tape player to the computer via a USB port and also software that would capture and enhance the sound recordings, many of which were already in poor condition. When these two were eventually sourced, it was discovered that an amplifier for boosting the signal from the tape player to the computer was also required for the workflow to occur as planned. Eventually, the necessary equipment and software were deployed for the program to begin its fledgling efforts.

Digitization efforts were boosted in 2008 when, through the generous donation of former University Librarian Mrs. Irma Goldstraw, the Digital Library Services Centre (DLSC) was established. With the acquisition of specialized equipment and the procurement of additional staff, the DLSC was able to collaborate almost immediately with OPReP on the project to digitize and reorganize the oral history recordings. Conversion of the OPReP tapes began in earnest and, to date, two hundred cassette tapes representing a total of 119 interviews have been converted to digital format. The interviews are backed up on DVDs and are also stored on one of the Alma Jordan Library's servers.

The transcripts of many of the interviews have also been submitted to the institutional repository, UWISpace, deployed by the library in August 2008 using the open-source DSpace platform. Dublin Core metadata records have been created to improve discoverability of these files via the web-based repository. The collection of transcripts can be browsed at http://uwispace.sta.uwi.edu/dspace/handle/2139/6340/.

The next step in the digitization project is to add audio clips of these recordings to UWISpace. It is anticipated that these will be made available to researchers once intellectual property rights and other legal issues have been clarified. Currently, the library offers two options for the assignment of literary property rights to materials in the oral history interviews: (a) the literary property rights may be retained by the interviewee until such time as he or she deems it appropriate to assign them to the library; (b) the literary property rights may be assigned immediately to the library. When literary property rights are assigned to the library, permission of the interviewee to quote it is not required, but the source must be acknowledged/cited by the researcher.

Publications

Spoken History

Spoken History is the original print guide to the material collected by the Oral and Pictorial Records Programme. Published in 1997, it was the product of the collaboration between Margaret Rouse-Jones, OPReP coordinator between 1983 and 1994 who created a legacy in building the program, and Mrs. Kathleen Helenese-Paul. The guide has been described as an "indispensable tool for researchers who need to be aware of this rich archive."[5]

OPReP Newsletter

The *OPReP Newsletter* is an extension of the program. Its publication began in 1988. It appeared quarterly up to 1994, and then bi-annually until December 2005, when it ceased due to staff constraints. Each issue of the newsletter carries a set format: there is a feature article, transcript excerpts of an interview relating to the article, and other miscellaneous items. The newsletter reported on the activities of the program and therefore served as a graphic reminder to the academic community and contributors that the program should be embraced for its role of "adding to the pool of historical and oral evidence about Trinidad and Tobago."[6]

In 2006, all the newsletters from 1988 to 2004 were scanned and became available on the library's webpage at http://www.mainlib.uwi.tt/divisions/wi/collmain/oprepweb/oprephome.htm. Here again there was a shift from a printed product to an online product, the 2005 publication having been issued only in an online format, thereby enhancing accessibility and visibility.

Lessons for Caribbean Libraries

There are many libraries in the Caribbean and elsewhere with similar collections of cassette tapes since this has been the standard procedure for gathering oral records. The digitization of oral history archives has to be well-thought-out. A digital laboratory, however rudimentary, with basic equipment and the required staffing is important. Apart from technical staff, there must be sufficient catalogers who can attach the metadata to the records in a timely manner, thereby facilitating their accessibility. Equipment needs to be versatile so that not only audiocassettes but videotapes and mini audiocassettes can also be converted. To a great extent, researchers are driving the process of moving to a mostly digital environment because with the advent of continually advancing technology, recordings are now created digitally. Appropriate software must also be taken into consideration and it is well advised to search the Internet for free software such as DSpace, which is an open-source tool.

This paper sought to give some insight into the process of converting one of the library's special collections from an analog to a digital format. There are many challenges but they are not insurmountable, and efforts continue to be unflagging in order to ensure that the initiative remains strong.

NOTES

1. Margaret Rouse-Jones and Enid Brown, "Documenting Cultural Heritage: The Oral History Collections at the University of the West Indies," in *Documenting Movements, Identity and Popular Culture in Latin America: Papers of the Forty-Fourth Annual Meeting of the Seminar on the Acquisition of Latin American Library Materials,* ed. Richard F. Phillips (Austin, Tex.: SALALM Secretariat, 2000). This paper explores in detail the history and development of the oral history programs at the St. Augustine and Mona campuses of the University of the West Indies.

2. The Main Library at the University of the West Indies, St. Augustine, was renamed the Alma Jordan Library and marked by a ceremony on February 28, 2011.

3. Margaret Rouse-Jones and Kathleen Helenese-Paul, introduction to *Spoken History: A Guide to the Material Collected by the Oral and Pictorial Records Programme* (St. Augustine: Main Library, University of the West Indies, 1997), 4.

4. Sir Ellis Clarke was the second and last Governor General of Trinidad and Tobago and the first President of the Republic of Trinidad and Tobago, 1976. He died on December 30, 2010.

5. Bridget Brereton, foreword to *Spoken History*, v.

6. Jamaica has two similar programs: the Social History Project, which is coordinated by the history department of the University of the West Indies at Mona, Jamaica; and the Memory Bank Project out of the Institute of Jamaica.

9. Archive It Old School:
Solo Collecting, Networking, and eBay

Claire-Lise Bénaud

"A library represents the mind of its collector, his fancies and foibles, his strength and weakness, his prejudices and preferences."[1] This quote by William Osler certainly holds true for poster collections. While collections have an intrinsic historical and cultural value of their own, learning how they were acquired provides an interesting facet that adds context to what is there, why, and how it made its way into a collection. In this study, I will discuss three poster collections acquired by collectors with three distinct collecting approaches: collecting on the run by David Holtby,[2] methodical and efficient networking by Sam L. Slick,[3] and buying on eBay by Ramón Figueroa.[4] Holtby focused on a single event—the Spanish general elections of 1977—and, as such, his collection covers this unique political moment. Slick collected broadly from all the Latin American countries as well as Spain, with posters representing such varied themes as elections, imperialism, solidarity, human rights, and revolution. Figueroa focused on Mexican film posters. The Holtby and Slick collections are housed at the University of New Mexico Libraries. Figueroa donated his film poster collection to the University of Florida in 2008 in honor of Efraín Barradas, his former professor and friend.

Collecting "On the Run"

David Holtby spent a year in Madrid as a Fulbright scholar, between September 1976 and August 1977, researching his dissertation on the Spanish civil war. His research did not focus on poster art even though he was familiar with the work of Spanish political poster artist Josep Renau. In June 1977, Spain held its first elections since the death of Francisco Franco in November 1975 and the first free elections in Spain since 1936. On May 1, 1977, May Day—a day not celebrated by the Franco regime—political posters spontaneously appeared all over town, especially in the subway stations. During the Franco regime, political posters had not been allowed. Holtby realized that this was a unique moment in history. Since campaigning on Spanish television and radio was still very controlled, and candidates were only allowed a limited amount of airtime, posters were a unique way to reach a mass audience. Even though putting up posters was spontaneous and part of a grassroots movement, printers and political parties were still required to register with a government agency.

In a 2005 lecture, Holtby explains how he got started.[5] He tells the story of how the poster *Fiesta de la Libertad* by José Ramón Sánchez inspired him to collect as many political posters as he could find. This particular poster appeared in early May 1977, weeks in advance of the official start of the twenty-one-day political campaign. One morning, near the metro's entrance by Madrid's Biblioteca Nacional, he came across about half a dozen people looking at this particular poster and heard an elderly woman, radiant with enthusiasm, say, "If we can celebrate liberty, we're really free, aren't we." This poster radiated a hope, a new sense of togetherness, a *convivencia* that drew people to it. The poster's theme—the exuberance, esprit, and joy borne of celebrating liberty—resonated deeply with people, himself included. It symbolized Spain's transition to democracy and the nation's recovery from its long, oppressive era.

Between May 1 and the day of the elections, June 15 (won by Adolfo Suárez, leader of the Unión de Centro Democrático), Holtby collected posters using a simple strategy. He would travel during the day on busy subway lines looking for posters and assessing which ones he would take. He picked the ones that did not have too much glue and therefore were easier to remove. Luckily, the walls of the subway were tiled and glue did not adhere well, so it was fairly easy to detach them. On his way home around 10:00 P.M., he would wait to make sure nobody was around and then take the posters he was interested in. He believed that militants put the posters up late at night or in the early mornings. He tried not to draw attention to himself. His fear was that militants would go after him if he removed one of their posters. He had memorized a few sentences ready to blurt out in case he would be confronted by someone. His apprehension was understandable since elections had taken place against a backdrop of demonstrations and some violence. Fortunately for the collection and himself, he never encountered any problems.

Holtby felt that being a foreign national, especially an American, was not a particularly popular thing at the time in Spain. The U.S. government had supported Franco's regime for many years and anti-American feelings were running high, so he did not want to be mistaken for a U.S. agent. After each taking, he was shaking. Holtby does not describe himself as a risktaker and had no experience dealing with militants. He also related how he dealt with the ethical questions posed by the "stealing" of election posters. He reasoned that since many identical posters were plastered on the walls, removing a single one did not negatively impact the message. Moreover, posters stayed on public display for a very short period of time anyway. Within a day or two, they were torn down or replaced by others. He could not wait too long to peel them off because new posters were plastered over the existing ones. As an American, he did not feel comfortable visiting political parties to collect posters directly, and he did not attend political rallies. In all, he collected some forty-five posters.

As a historian, Holtby knew he had to collect posters from all groups, from the far right to the far left in order to give his collection historical validity. Some posters were about particular issues such as Basque groups, anarchist groups, and leftist groups. This coverage makes the collection more valuable and interesting. Holtby collected them the way the Spaniards posted them: on the run.

Collecting Systematically

Sam Slick, a professor at Sam Houston State University and later at the University of Southern Mississippi, collected posters with a clear purpose: to use in teaching. Interestingly enough, his collecting also started with Spain: he asked a colleague who was going to Spain in the mid-1970s to bring back posters to the United States. This colleague returned with forty or fifty posters that formed the basis of his archive. He became captivated with posters as visual, textual, and political documents. In 1976 Slick founded the International Archives of Latin American Political Posters (IALAPP); he also built an adjunct archive to IALAPP consisting of Spanish political posters from the post-Franco era.

Over the next quarter century, he collected over twelve thousand posters from the twenty-two countries of Latin America and Spain. The archives document contemporary Latin America, covering a broad range of topics including social problems and popular graphic art but with an emphasis on political election posters. For a detailed description of this archive, see my earlier article "Latin American and Iberian Posters: The Sam Slick Collection at the University of New Mexico."[6] Slick found the posters stimulating and interesting and a good way to study and teach politics and cultural life, but he also realized that he was saving an ephemeral artifact and was preserving a distinct genre.

Professor Slick soon developed a systematic strategy for collecting posters and built a network of contacts in Latin America and Spain. He contacted cultural attachés in the United States; he asked his Latin American graduate students to collect posters while visiting home; and he also asked them to write to their families for help. Often these students were from well-off families and were able to send their maids to political offices to collect posters. He also collected posters on his own trips, establishing good connections with government offices and personal connections with graphic artists. He participated in seminars dealing with Latin American posters, including SALALM, and traveled and spread the word about his collection. The only exception to this approach was the Cuban posters, which he obtained directly from Cuban government agencies. The specific way he acquired Cuban posters is covered in more detail in a previous SALALM conference paper titled "A Poster Is Worth 10,000 Words: Cuban Political Posters at the University of New Mexico."[7]

Collecting on eBay

Ramón A. Figueroa, currently associate professor of Spanish at Millsaps College in Jackson, Mississippi, began collecting Mexican film posters in 1994. His collecting was a confluence of two interests: Mexican culture and a passion for collecting. As a native of the Dominican Republic, he grew up with Mexican soap operas, comics, music, and film.[8] He visited Mexico in 1989 and fell in love with the country. Figueroa was always a collector. He collected books, records, Mexican masks, and pottery, and he became interested in collecting art—but he could not afford it. Poster art was the answer. He was inspired by his friend and mentor Efraín Barradas, a disciplined and experienced collector of Puerto Rican posters. Barradas told him "you learn to love what you can afford."[9] This proved true for Figueroa.

He started collecting on eBay. His strategy was straightforward. He would start with a broad search for "Mexican posters," which never produced overwhelming results. Normally, from a result of three hundred items at most, he could easily narrow his search to movie posters. Since the Mexican movie industry went into decline in the 1960s, he restricted his collecting to the golden age of Mexican cinema covering the 1940s and 1950s. Figueroa's motivation was purely aesthetic. What interested him most was the beauty of the poster rather than specific movie stars, directors, or poster artists. He found that in general, though, the better movies with the most famous stars had the best posters. Figueroa stated that the artistic quality of the Mexican movie posters of this era was much higher than their American counterparts, because in Mexico the posters were created by artists whereas in the United States they were created by illustrators.

The collection spotlights the work of many of the great actors and actresses of the era (for example, María Félix, Pedro Infante, Pedro Armendáriz, Ricardo Montalbán, Tin-Tan, Alicia Alonso, Carlos Cruz, and Jorge Martínez), film directors (for example, Luis Buñuel, Miguel M. Delgado, Joaquín Pardavé, Juan Orol, Leopoldo Laborde, Daniel Díaz Torres, Luis Felipe Bernaza, Mario Rivas, and Enrique Pineda Barnet), and renowned poster artists (for example, Alberto Vargas, Eduardo Muñoz Bachs, Josep Renau, Ernesto García Cabral, Leopoldo Mendoza, and Antonio Fernández Reboiro).

Between 1994 and 2005, Figueroa checked eBay many times daily and most of his purchases were through bidding. He learned to read eBay descriptions carefully and was always aware of the condition of the posters: whether they had holes, rips, or other imperfections, even when they did not show in the eBay picture. The vast majority of posters of that era were not in mint condition, and he said that usually the sellers' descriptions were truthful. Typically, they were printed on poor quality paper and are now brittle. Depending on the image and the condition, prices ranged from a low of $10 to an average of $25 or $30. A few select ones, for example, a Buñuel poster, could go as high as $700 or $800, but these were the exception rather than the rule. The relatively low prices are a reflection of the lack of interest in Mexican movie posters by American collectors.

Sellers of Mexican movie posters constitute a rather small group of people with a keen interest in Mexican cinema. Most of them have a Mexican connection, either through their background, family relations, or even the Mexican movie industry. For example, one seller was the son of a movie actor from this time period. Figueroa believes that the best Mexican film poster collections are in the United States, either in universities or private collections such as the Agrasánchez Film Archive.

Figueroa collected but did not have a methodical way of organizing or displaying his collection. He kept it under his bed. As a result, he could not easily keep track of what he had and even purchased some duplicates. In the fall of 2008, he donated 378 film posters to the Department of Special and Area Studies Collections at the George A. Smathers Libraries at the University of Florida in Gainesville, where they were preserved, digitized, and made available for public viewing.

Preservation

The posters collected by Holtby and Figueroa have been scanned and are available online in the New Mexico Digital Collections at the University of New Mexico, and in the University of Florida Digital Collections, respectively. Slick's posters are currently being digitized. All three collections needed preservation work. The physical preservation of the posters collected by Holtby was problematic since many had excessive glue slopped over them. Holtby simply bought tubes and brought the posters back with him to the United States, where they were flattened and placed in map cases. Similarly, Slick received posters in tubes, flattened them, marked them, and placed them in map cases, but these posters were in very good condition. Many of Figueroa's film posters were brittle and needed cosmetic repairs before being encapsulated.

Conclusion

These three collections reflect different motivations, interests, and approaches to a process that in the end produces a similar result. Like all other creative endeavors, collecting, and especially collecting something as ephemeral as posters, reflects the individual's own personal style. Opportunity, availability, and chance play a crucial role in what ends up in library collections. While Holtby reflected on piracy, I do not know if Slick or Figueroa considered who owns posters, who can use them, why, and for what purpose. Do poster collectors struggle at all with taking or purchasing pieces that belong to a country's cultural heritage?

Historian David Holtby was present in a unique political moment documented through its propaganda, via a transitory medium not designed to preserve history. His action preserved this unique record of a tumultuous and brief period of political transition. Without the historian's eye, the posters might have only appealed as novelties to someone interested in a strictly political point of view. His attempt at even coverage of all sides of the issue—left, right, center, anarchists, nationalists—offered a truly vivid picture of the energy that existed at the time.

Collecting posters was Sam Slick's passion, and he did it throughout his career. Slick used his posters for educational and pedagogical purposes and tried to gather as large a swath of this cultural and social output as he could. He cast a wide net and his collection reflects the communal intellectual production of an era. Organizations and individuals who create posters do them for a specific event, not for documenting history for the future and this, paradoxically, makes their historical importance so unique. Just by chance, there is no duplication of posters between Holtby's and Slick's collections. Holtby, a small collector, filled out a major part of Spanish history.

Ramón Figueroa's interest in Mexican movies from the golden age produced a collection of posters that most likely, if not gathered systematically, would have deteriorated and disappeared from the cultural record. His private interest in Mexican movie posters renders the same significance to a nonpolitical activity as the other two collections do for politics, history, and culture. Like political events, movies are "a moment in time." Yet, like the first free elections in a newly democratic country, or the various social or cultural reforms initiated by governments, they are part of the intellectual and cultural discourse of a society. The posters condense the message and become a propaganda tool of their own.

These three very different collections, gathered by such different methods and for such different purposes, illustrate the importance posters play in the political, social, and cultural life of a society. Whether effective propaganda tools or illusion, they capture a mode of thinking in a specific moment in time.

NOTES

1. Quote from William Osler, http://thinkexist.com/quotes.

2. David Holtby is Senior Program Manager, Center for Regional Studies, Zimmerman Library, University of New Mexico. He donated his Spanish poster collection to the University of New Mexico Libraries in the spring of 2007. I interviewed him on February 23, 2010.

3. Sam L. Slick is a collector, scholar, and former Spanish professor at the University of Southern Mississippi. The University of New Mexico Libraries acquired his collection in 2001. I interviewed him on May 2, 2002.

4. Ramón Figueroa is Associate Professor of Spanish at Millsaps College in Mississippi.

5. David V. Holtby, "The Art of Democracy: Fifty Years of Spain's Political Posters (1930s–1980s)," (lecture, Zimmerman Library, University of New Mexico, July 15, 2005).

6. Claire-Lise Bénaud, "Latin American and Iberian Posters: The Sam Slick Collection at the University of New Mexico," *Collection Management* 27, no. 2 (2002): 87–95.

7. Claire-Lise Bénaud and Sharon A. Moynahan, "A Poster Is Worth 10,000 Words: Cuban Political Posters at the University of New Mexico," in *Trends and Traditions in Latin American and Caribbean History,* ed. Denise A. Hibay (Austin, Tex.: SALALM Secretariat, 2005), 61–68.

8. See Department of Special and Area Studies Collections, George A. Smathers Libraries, University of Florida in Gainesville, http://dloc.com/ufdc/?m=hitfilmposters.

9. Ramón Figueroa, interview by the author, July 2, 2010.

10. The Cuban Collections of the Library of Congress: An Overview

Georgette M. Dorn

Introduction

The Library of Congress holds arguably one of the most comprehensive collections of book and nonbook materials on Cuba. The Library of Congress (LC) began collecting materials relating to Cuba in the middle of the nineteenth century, when the United States sought markets in the Caribbean, and has continued to the present. Despite the U.S. embargo, since 1960 LC has maintained exchange relations with the National Library of Cuba and the University of Havana. The Hispanic Division's chief, Howard F. Cline, fostered scholarly cooperation with Cuban academics in the 1960s, especially after he founded the Latin American Studies Association in 1966 with a group of prominent U.S. Latin Americanists.

The primary point of access for Cuban materials as well as for the Luso-Hispanic and Caribbean collections at the Library of Congress is via the Hispanic Reading Room. Electronic access as well as descriptive information is available via the Hispanic Reading Room webpage (www.loc.gov/rr/hispanic). The reference staff and area specialists are also available by telephone. Access to LC's online catalog is at http://catalog.loc.gov/.

Bibliographies

An indispensable source for books and periodicals about Cuba is the *Handbook of Latin American Studies,* an annual, selective, annotated, and scholarly bibliography in the humanities and social sciences prepared by an editorial staff in the Hispanic Division and published by the University of Texas Press in Austin. Volume 65 (social sciences) will be published in 2010. The volume on the humanities is due out in 2011. The entire handbook, which began in 1935, is also available online at http://lcweb2.loc.gov/hlas/.

In April 1970, Howard F. Cline, the then director of the Hispanic Foundation (renamed Hispanic Division in 1978), with support by the Ford Foundation, convened an international conference that focused on collecting Cuban materials. The proceedings of the conference were published in 1970 in *Cuban Acquisitions and Bibliography,* compiled and edited by Earl J. Pariseau. This important work also mentions other significant Cuban collections in Spain and the United Kingdom.

Roberto Esquenazi Mayo, then visiting professor at Georgetown University, compiled a comprehensive overview of Cuban periodicals in the library in his *Survey of Cuban Revistas, 1902–1958.*

The General Collection

The general collection includes LC's holdings of books, bound periodicals, and microfilms. Cuban history, society, culture, and the arts, as well as the basic sciences are well represented in the general collection: the most important works on those subject areas in any language can be found here.

Within the general collection some unique holdings are worth highlighting. The colonial period (1492–1898) is uniquely represented in contemporary chronicles about the Spanish Indies and in Spain's government reports. Examples of important early accounts include Felipe Poey y Aloy's *Geografía física y política de la isla de Cuba* (1857) and *Memorias sobre la historia natural de la isla de Cuba* (1861), and Jacobo de la Pezuela y Lobo's *Crónica de las Antillas* (1871) and *Historia de la isla de Cuba* (1868–1878). Also available are all the works of historian and sociologist José Antonio Saco and historian Felipe Poey y Aloy.

Coverage of the Ten Years' War of 1868–1878, which sought Cuba's independence, encompasses history, politics, society, and literature. Enrique Collazo explains the defeat of the revolutionaries in *Desde Yara hasta el Zanjón, apuntaciones históricas* (1893); equally relevant are works by Francisco Javier Cisneros, Fermín Valdés Domínguez, Antonio Zambrana, Miguel Aldama, and Carlos Manuel de Céspedes. Among other materials are several firsthand accounts of the participants such as Carlos Manuel de Céspedes, Manuel de la Cruz, Máximo Gómez, and Juan V. Escalera.

The collection covering the 1895–1898 period includes firsthand accounts by U.S. officials, Cubans, and Spaniards. Also among these are writings by Cuban poet José Martí, Máximo Gómez, and several journalists. Biographies of key actors are all here, including Antonio Maceo and other leaders. There is also the *Inventario general del Archivo de la Delegación del Partido Revolucionario Cubano,* which covers the publications of Cuban leaders who lived in New York City in the last quarter of the nineteenth century. The Spanish side of the war is also well documented, and the collection includes important historical works by U.S. authors.

The collections of items published after Cuba achieved its independence cover all aspects of the country's history, society, and culture. Most works are in Spanish and in English, but many are in other languages. The collection has, for example, books published in Russian between 1960 and 1989, a period during which Cuba had a special relationship with the Soviet Union. The 1920–1950s period is well covered, but LC's holdings from 1959 to the present are second to none. All the major authors are represented including Herminio Portell Vilá, Emilio Roig de Leuchsenring, Leo S. Rowe, Russell Fitzgibbon,

Manuel Moreno Fraginals, Hugh Thomas, Theodore Draper, Carlos Franqui, Huber Matos, Edward González, Carlos Alberto Montaner, and others. There are many biographies of Fidel Castro and Ernesto (Che) Guevara. Also worth noting are the pathbreaking studies on Afro-Cuban society and culture by Fernando Ortíz and Lydia Cabrera.

U.S. foreign policy is well documented in primary sources and secondary publications as is the Cuban diaspora in the United States. The Hispanic Division recently purchased the entire collection of microfilms of the Cuban Heritage Collection of Cuban Radio Broadcasts for the 1962–1982 period.

For Cuba as for the rest of the Iberian world, literature presents special insights into a country's society and culture. The collection of Cuban literature is truly outstanding. Major literary figures whose complete works are represented in the collections include José Martí, José Lezama Lima, Alejo Carpentier, Reinaldo Arenas, Eliseo Diego, Nicolás Guillén, Cintio Vitier, Heberto Padilla, Lisandro Otero, Pablo Armando Fernández, and many others. Holdings of literary and cultural periodicals are also outstanding. Esquenazi Mayo's *Survey of Cuban Revistas* presents a thorough analysis of Cuban cultural periodicals between 1902 and 1958.

Rare Books

The collection houses rare published documents and books relating to the colonial period, independence, and beyond. Among the many unique items is included a twelve-page document published in 1799 to allow horse breeding in Cuba. There is the 1810 proclamation, entitled *Fidelísimos habitantes de la isla de Cuba,* by the island's governor, the Marqués de Someruelos, pledging the island's loyalty to the Spanish Crown during the time when most Spanish colonies in Latin America initiated independence movements. Also available are a rare copy of the 1813 constitution of Cuba, published in Cádiz, Spain, which never went into effect; an 1846 description of a devastating hurricane; Thomas William Wilson's *Authentic Narrative of the Piratical Descents upon Cuba...*(1851); and Richard Burleigh Kimball's *Cuba and the Cubans* (1850).

The rare books collection also houses broadsides and official publications, including the U.S. Senate document proclaiming the independence of Cuba on December 21, 1896. A unique collection is the handcrafted publications of poetry, music, and art by Ediciones Vigía, a publishing house founded in 1984 in the city of Matanzas by writers, musicians, and composers. Vigía represented an unusual concession by the Cuban government, which allowed this somewhat controversial small press to flourish.

Manuscripts

Although the Manuscript Division houses for the most part U.S. archival materials, including the papers of almost all U.S. presidents up to Herbert

Hoover, Latin American countries are also represented, especially Mexico and to a certain extent Cuba.

An interesting set of documents resides in the Domingo Del Monte Collection. Several items concern the defense of Santiago de Cuba against a British expedition in 1782 and measures taken by Spain to defend its possessions (1805). There are papers dealing with the antislavery movement and abolition of the slave trade (1805–1868), including letters of Cuban poet and son of slaves Francisco Manzano (1797–1857), whose freedom was bought by Domingo Del Monte y Aponte and his friends. Incidentally, this collection was donated by the wealthy Cuban writer, historian, lawyer, and collector Domingo Del Monte (1804–1853), who was born in Venezuela of Dominican parents but left the island after being indicted for his abolitionist activities. The Del Monte collection of historical documents about Cuba and other areas of the Caribbean ranges from 1597 through 1829; many are official reports of governor-generals and captain-generals, information about colonization, administration, slave trade, military affairs, and copper mining, among other topics.

The Papers of General Leonard Wood (1860–1927), who served in the U.S. Army in the Spanish-American War and became governor of Cuba, were also donated to the library and are major research resources for 1898 and early Cuban independence and nationhood.

José Ignacio Rodríguez (1831–1907), international lawyer and important political figure, donated his valuable collection to the library. He spent many years in the United States after he was exiled from his country in 1869 for his revolutionary activities. This collection is LC's largest Cuban manuscript collection. Covering the 1853–1907 period, it contains letters from many Cuban political figures who shaped the reformist and the independence movements, as well as the papers of the Cuban Junta of New York for 1868–1870 and the archive of the Real Sociedad de Amigos del País in Havana.

Many other collections contain materials relating to Cuba, among these, ship logs by sea captains, as well as documents of American diplomats and other government officials such as the papers of Secretaries of State John Hay (1899–1905), Elihu Root (1905–1908), and Philander Knox (1909–1913). The papers of Presidents Theodore Roosevelt, William Howard Taft, and Woodrow Wilson also contain important documents relevant to the island's history.

The Recorded Sound Collections

The Hispanic Division has recorded 28 Cuban writers from the 1950s to the present for the Archive of Hispanic Literature on Tape. This unique archive, begun in 1943, boasts a collection of recordings by 660 Latin American, Caribbean, Iberian, and Hispanic American writers.

The outstanding Afro-Cuban poet Nicolás Guillén was recorded in 1958 by Francisco Aguilera, then specialist in Hispanic Culture. Reinaldo Arenas read for the archive the week after he arrived in the United States through the Mariel boatlift. Guillermo Cabrera Infante was videotaped for the archive in 1985. Additional writers included are Juan José Arrom, Miguel Barnet, Antonio Benítez Rojo, Lydia Cabrera, Julieta Campos, Lourdes Casal, Angel Cuadra, Belkis Cuza Malé, Edmundo Desnoes, Eliseo Diego, Pablo Armando Fernández, Eugenio Florit, Carlos Franqui, Nancy Morejón, Heberto Padilla, Hilda Perera, Juana Pita, Eliana Rivero, Severo Sarduy (recorded by this writer in Paris), José Triana (recorded by this writer in San Juan, Puerto Rico), Odilio Urfé, Roberto Valero, and Armando Valladares.

The American Folklife Center (formerly the Archive of Folk Song) recorded Cuban music and culture from the 1920s onward. Some of these are wire-recordings; others are on reel-to-reel tapes or long-playing records. This collection has a set of long-playing records, *Música de los cultos africanos en Cuba,* published in Havana and compiled by the renowned folklorist and anthropologist Lydia Cabrera.

In addition, the Recorded Sound Reference Center houses hundreds of hours of recorded radio addresses by Fidel Castro, transferred to the library from other U.S. government agencies.

The Geography and Map Collection

According to John Hébert, chief of the Geography and Map Division, Cuba is the best-mapped country in the hemisphere. During the early modern period, Spain and Portugal led the world in the areas of navigation and mapmaking. From 1507 onward, the Spanish Crown began to assemble maps, geographic data, plans, and nautical charts for the Atlantic and African worlds. Cuba was one of the earliest outposts of the Spanish Atlantic Empire, so it is no surprise that it is indeed well mapped.

The library's collection of maps depicting Cuba is the largest in the world. Four colonial era items of note depict Cuba exclusively, among these, the 1665–1670 maps of the island by the Dutch cartographer Joan Vinckeboons. An early manuscript map of Guantanamo Bay is the "Plano de la Bahia de Guantamo en la Isla de Cuba" (1751). According to John Hébert's *Luso-Hispanic World in Maps: A Selective Guide to Manuscript Maps to 1900 in the Collections of the Library of Congress*, the library has more than eighty manuscript maps specifically relating to Cuba or topographic areas of the island.

Cuba's coastline and ports were well mapped in nautical charts from the colonial period through the entire nineteenth century. One example is a British manuscript map, "A Plan of the Entrance and Fortifications of the Harbour of Saint Iago on the South Side of Cuba," by Captain Phil Durell (1741), which provided an entry to the city of Santiago de Cuba.

According to the 1970 work *Cuban Acquisitions and Bibliography* mentioned above, maps covering geographic regions, provincial maps, are very useful because of their comparative scale and detail. LC has subject maps, for instance, of mining, public works, agriculture, and telecommunications. Municipal maps of cities and towns were created by the Cuban Cartographic Service in 1952 and 1953. Other items of special interest are the Sanborn Fire Insurance Company Maps for Cuba for the 1900–1950 period, which include an online index.

Mention should also be made of recent maps created by satellite and transferred to LC by other federal agencies.

Prints and Photographs

Alan Fern, former chief in the Prints and Photographs Division, wrote in *Cuban Acquisitions and Bibliography* that prints, cartoons, posters, and other visual materials relating to Cuba form a significant and unique part of LC's Cuban holdings.

The Spanish-American War of 1898 and its immediate aftermath are well represented in several collections housed in the Prints and Photographs collection. Of special interest are depictions of roads, bridges, buildings, and tourist card views. The early twentieth century, when U.S. economic and political interest in Cuba was intense, is particularly well represented and includes posters, political cartoons, and photographs. There is a stereoscopic photographs collection (from about 1900), which depicts Cuba and the Spanish-American War.

The Archive of Hispanic Culture collection, which was assembled from 1940 to 1944 through a Rockefeller Foundation grant, contains photographs, negatives, lithographs, records of architecture, historic buildings, sculptures, and decorative and graphic arts.

The 1962 missile crisis can be viewed in photographs of the missile bases that the Soviet Union installed in Cuba. Additionally, the post-revolutionary Cuban government has encouraged the production of posters on arts, culture, and politics, and the library has acquired a significant sample of these materials.

The portrait collection includes representations of notable Cuban personalities in politics, the arts, and the sciences. Included here are two portraits of famous ballerina Alicia Alonso, several of independence leaders Antonio Maceo and José Martí, and of Cuba's first president, Tomás Estrada Palma.

The Music Collection

Most of the important books and scores on Cuban music are housed in the Music Division. Of special interest in this collection are two holograph scores by two major Cuban composers, Julián Orbon and Aurelio de la Vega, as well as some correspondence from Cuban musicians.

Books range from the general studies of Cuban music and musical life to specific studies, such as Edwin Tuerbe Colón's *Operas cubanas y sus autores* (1943), Alejo Carpentier's *La música en Cuba* (1946), and José Ardévol's *Música y revolución* (1966).

However, it is in popular music that Cuba is most renowned, and since the late nineteenth century it continues enjoying great popularity beyond the country's borders. Combining African, Spanish, and Caribbean rhythms, Cuban musicians gave birth to the *trova* (which began with itinerant musicians), the *son,* rumba, mambo, and Cuban jazz. They also developed their own version of bolero, among others. All these genres are well represented in the Recorded Sound Collection.

The great innovators of the twentieth century, among them Ernesto Lecuona (who composed *Siboney*), Manuel Barruero, Amadeo Roldán, and Gonzalo Roig, are also represented in this collection. After the Cuban Revolution, many contemporary practitioners emigrated. Among them were salsa singer Celia Cruz, Cachao, La Lupe, and Gloria Estefan, as well as the great classical guitarist and composer Leo Brower, who is still in Cuba and is well represented with 134 works.

In the American Folklife Center, there are Afro-Cuban social dances recorded in the 1930s and the set of long-playing records entitled *Música de los cultos africanos en Cuba.*

BIBLIOGRAPHY

Ardévol, José. *Música y revolución.* La Habana: Unión de Escritores y Artistas de Cuba, 1966.

Carpentier, Alejo. *La música en Cuba.* Mexico: Fondo de Cultura Económica, 1946.

Collazo, Enrique. *Desde Yara hasta el Zanjón: Apuntaciones históricas.* La Habana: Tip. de "La Lucha," 1893.

Esquenazi Mayo, Roberto. *A Survey of Cuban Revistas, 1902–1958.* Washington, D.C.: Library of Congress, 1993.

Hébert, John R., and Anthony P. Mullan. *The Luso-Hispanic World in Maps: A Selective Guide to Manuscript Maps to 1900 in the Collections of the Library of Congress.* Washington, D.C.: Library of Congress, 1999.

Inventario general del archivo de la delegación del Partido Revolucionario Cubano en Nueva York (1892–1898). La Habana: Impr. "El Siglo XX," Sociedad Editorial Cuba Contemporánea, 1918.

Kimball, Richard B., C. F. Madan, and J. A. Saco. *Cuba and the Cubans: Comprising a History of the Island of Cuba, Its Present, Social, Political, and Domestic Condition; Also, Its Relation to England and the United States.* New York: S. Hueston, 1850.

Muro y Salazar, Salvador, marqués de Someruelos. *Fidelísimos habitantes de la Isla de Cuba.* La Habana: Imprenta de la Capitanía General, 1810.

O'Farrill y Herrera, José Ricardo. *Gracia concedida por S.M. á los habitantes de esta isla para la introducción de caballos frisones de ambos sexos, desde las provincias del Norte de América.* La Habana: Imprenta de la Capitanía General, 1799.

Pariseau, Earl J., comp. *Cuban Acquisitions and Bibliography: Proceedings and Working Papers of an International Conference Held at the Library of Congress, April 13–15, 1970.* Washington, D.C.: Library of Congress, 1970.

Pezuela, Jacobo de la. *Crónica de las Antillas.* Madrid: Rubio, Grilo y Vitturi, 1871.

———. *Historia de la isla de Cuba.* 4 vols. Madrid: C. Bailly-Baillière; Nueva York: Baillière Hermanos, 1868–1878.

Poey, Felipe. *Geografía física y política de la isla de Cuba.* La Habana: Imprenta de la viuda de Barcina, 1857.

———. *Memorias sobre la historia natural de la isla de Cuba: Acompañadas de sumarios latinos y extractos en francés.* La Habana: Imprenta de Barcina, 1861.

Tolón, Edwin T., and Jorge A. González. *Operas cubanas y sus autores.* La Habana: Imprenta Ucar, García, 1943.

Wilson, Thomas W. *An Authentic Narrative of the Piratical Descents upon Cuba Made by Hordes from the United States Headed by Narciso López, a Native of South America: To Which Are Added Some Interesting Letters and Declarations from the Prisoners, with a List of Their Names &c.* La Habana: [s.n.], 1851.

11. Contenidos latinoamericanos en revistas españolas: dificultades para determinar la colección de publicaciones de estudios latinoamericanos

Luis Rodríguez Yunta

Introducción

Las revistas científicas juegan un rol fundamental en los procesos de comunicación científica. La irrupción de la edición electrónica conlleva facilidades hasta ahora desconocidas para divulgar trabajos fuera de los circuitos tradicionales, limitados a las suscripciones individuales y a la consulta en bibliotecas. Las publicaciones electrónicas periódicas pueden llegar a un número considerablemente más amplio de lectores, pero también compiten con la inflación de documentos disponibles en repositorios o páginas institucionales y personales. En consecuencia, las revistas pueden perder su preponderancia entre las publicaciones académicas si no se refuerza su función de filtro de calidad a través de los procesos de evaluación por pares. Por ello, actualmente se manifiestan tendencias algo contradictorias: por un lado surgen depósitos libres de documentos y nuevos títulos con poco rigor en sus criterios editoriales, por otro lado se acrecienta la presión por la evaluación de la calidad para determinar colecciones de élite que garanticen el nivel de contenido científico.

Para las bibliotecas académicas y centros de documentación, la atención a las publicaciones periódicas continúa siendo una práctica esencial. La gestión de colecciones está dando paso a la administración de recursos electrónicos de carácter muy diferente. Las revistas se clasifican habitualmente por disciplinas y subdisciplinas científicas y, en este sentido, cumplen una función esencial para identificar campos de trabajo y comunidades de investigadores. La ampliación de la colección física a la virtual, lejos de liberar a los profesionales del control de la colección ha complicado cada vez más su labor. Sigue siendo esencial poder determinar la lista más completa posible de títulos relevantes sobre un área disciplinaria, y al mismo tiempo poder diferenciar cuáles son los más esenciales. Y para ello debe contemplarse tanto las publicaciones que aún se editan exclusivamente en formato impreso, como las electrónicas o las que tienen doble formato, con sus diferentes condiciones de acceso.

Los estudios regionales son un ámbito de especial dificultad, por su carácter multidisciplinario, debido a que en ellos se pueden clasificar publicaciones de carácter general junto a otras muy especializadas. El área disciplinaria no siempre queda bien definida y se producen zonas difusas que generan dudas en los sistemas de clasificación de revistas. La investigación sobre Latinoamérica cuenta con una tradición importante en España, la cual permite identificar un conjunto de revistas con niveles aceptables de calidad e internacionalidad.[1] Sin embargo, no resulta fácil precisar el número de títulos que lo componen, puesto que junto a las publicaciones específicas, conviven otros títulos de interés parcial que deben tenerse también en cuenta.[2] En este sentido, en esta comunicación se plantean los problemas encontrados en la categorización de las revistas españolas para determinar la colección de publicaciones especializadas en estudios latinoamericanos, a partir de diferentes fuentes en las que se colabora desde los servicios de documentación del CSIC.

Las revistas españolas de estudios latinoamericanos en ISOC, Latindex y portales de REDIAL

Desde los años ochenta, el Consejo Superior de Investigaciones Científicas (CSIC) actualiza y distribuye tres bases de datos en línea que reflejan la producción científica española, especialmente en artículos de revistas científicas: ISOC (especializada en Ciencias Sociales y Humanas), ICYT (Ciencia y Tecnología) e IME (Ciencias de la Salud).[3] Estos ficheros se constituyeron a partir de los repertorios bibliográficos iniciados en los años setenta: Índice Médico Español, Índice Español de Ciencias Sociales, Índice Español de Humanidades e Índice Español de Ciencia y Tecnología. Vinculado a estos productos se ofrece la consulta de directorios de las revistas analizadas en estas bases de datos bibliográficas. Entre ellos, el Directorio de Revistas Españolas de Ciencias Sociales y Humanas, asociado a la base de datos ISOC, contempla la etiqueta América Latina dentro de sus áreas temáticas.[4] Estas adscripciones disciplinarias corresponden con el primer nivel jerárquico en el sistema de clasificación de la base bibliográfica de artículos. Este nivel se emplea para la subdivisión de ISOC en diferentes ficheros que pueden consultarse de forma independiente: América Latina, Antropología, Arqueología, Bellas Artes, etc. De esta manera, la clasificación "América Latina" se asigna no solo a las publicaciones sino también a los artículos y documentos vaciados, para conformar el fondo de referencias de la subbase ISOC-América Latina.

En el Directorio de Revistas Españolas de Ciencias Sociales y Humanas de las bases de datos del CSIC están incluidas actualmente cincuenta y siete revistas consideradas dentro del área temática América Latina. De las cuales, dieciséis títulos figuran como publicaciones muertas que ya no se editan y cuarenta y una como vivas. Puede determinarse que las revistas clasificadas en esta categoría definen el núcleo básico de revistas que alimentan la subbase ISOC-América Latina, aunque en este fichero se incluye también cualquier artículo relativo a estos estudios regionales independientemente de la publicación en la que haya sido editado. En la tabla 1 se compara el tamaño de esta subbase en

Tabla 1. División temática de las subbases ISOC,
revistas vivas y número de documentos vaciados editados
en el periodo 2008-2009.

Subbases ISOC (ejemplos)	Revistas vivas	N° documentos 2008/09
América Latina	41	**2329**
Antropología	35	**716**
Arqueología	90	**1201**
Educación	159	**3533**
Derecho	195	**4127**
Historia	228	**3535**
Lengua y Literatura	231	**4076**
Psicología	109	**2456**
Sociología y Políticas	132	**2658**

Fuente: Base de datos ISOC 2010.

relación con otros ficheros que ofrece la base ISOC. Puede corroborarse que aunque en el número de revistas se sitúa dentro de las agrupaciones de menor tamaño, sí ocupa un nivel intermedio por número de artículos. Esto se debe a la aportación de los artículos presentes en numerosas publicaciones clasificadas en todas las disciplinas.

El trabajo desarrollado por el CSIC en la selección de publicaciones científicas nacionales, ha facilitado su participación desde 1998 en la agrupación iberoamericana Latindex, aportando los datos sobre revistas españolas.[5] Latindex ha desarrollado un sistema consensuado de evaluación en base a 33 parámetros de calidad editorial. Actualmente ofrece tres recursos de información: el Directorio, que reúne datos bibliográficos de todas las revistas que cumplen los criterios mínimos, el Catálogo, que incluye únicamente las revistas que superan un umbral superior de criterios de calidad, y el Enlace a Revistas Electrónicas, que permite identificar las publicaciones que ofrecen acceso a los textos completos en Internet.

En el sistema Latindex las publicaciones están clasificadas por el área disciplinaria en la que se inscriben. En el primer nivel de la clasificación solo se incluyen grandes conjuntos, Artes y Humanidades, Ciencias Agrarias, Ingenierías, Ciencias Exactas y Naturales, Ciencias Médicas y Ciencias Sociales. Solo dentro de este último grupo se contempla como subtema la entrada Estudios Latinoamericanos. En ella existen 138 títulos en el directorio, de los cuales cuarenta y cinco son editados en España. También en este caso hay algunas revistas ya muertas, de modo que las vigentes suponen cuarenta y un publicaciones. En el catálogo han entrado veintitrés de ellas, de forma que puede considerarse que este subconjunto define el núcleo principal de las revistas españolas especializadas en América Latina con un mayor rigor en el cumplimiento de los indicadores de calidad editorial fijados por Latindex.

Este sistema iberoamericano permite distinguir las publicaciones que cumplen con los protocolos de buenas prácticas editoriales, pero estos criterios no permiten establecer filtros más estrictos de categorización de las revistas. Los indicadores establecidos son pautas que todas las publicaciones pueden llegar a cumplir. Sin embargo, las agencias nacionales de evaluación demandan criterios más selectivos para valorar el currículo de los investigadores. También las bibliotecas y los productores de las principales bases de datos internacionales precisan establecer criterios de selección de las fuentes que constituyen su colección. Por ello, en el CSIC, el Grupo de Investigación de Evaluación de Publicaciones Científicas (EPUC) realizó encuestas específicas a los investigadores españoles y estudios complementarios de citación, para poder establecer un sistema de categorización de las revistas españolas.[6]

La base de datos ISOC aplica desde 2006 un sistema basado en estos datos en su política de selección de publicaciones fuente.[7] Como resultado de esta evaluación, las publicaciones se dividen en categorías que expresan tanto la calidad editorial como el prestigio entre los investigadores españoles. De las cincuenta y siete revistas consideradas en los Estudios Latinoamericanos, solo tres se sitúan en la clase A (muy alta) y dos en la B (alta).[8] De estas cinco publicaciones principales, dos pertenecen al CSIC (*Anuario de Estudios Americanos* y *Revista de Indias*) y tres a la Universidad Complutense de Madrid (*Anales de Literatura Hispanoamericana, Revista Complutense de Historia de América* y *Revista Española de Antropología Americana*). Otras treinta revistas se sitúan en la clase C, conformando en total un conjunto de treinta y cinco publicaciones. Restando cuatro casos de revistas ya muertas, quedan en treinta y una el núcleo básico con el que en este momento se actualizan las referencias en la subbase de datos ISOC-América Latina. En este grupo entran las veintitrés publicaciones que Latindex incluye en su catálogo con la clasificación de Estudios Latinoamericanos, aunado a cinco casos que solo están en el directorio y otras revistas que figuran asignadas a otras disciplinas.

Además de participar en Latindex, el CSIC colabora asimismo en la Red Europea de Información y Documentación Científica (REDIAL). Se trata de una asociación de instituciones europeas que ofrecen recursos para los estudios latinoamericanos en Europa. Desde esta red, el CSIC colabora en dos portales de información, uno de ámbito nacional (Americanismo.es) y otro europeo (América Latina Portal Europeo).[9] Ambos sistemas comparten contenidos e incluyen un catálogo de publicaciones latinoamericanistas. La información contenida en Americanismo.es se refiere específicamente a los estudios latinoamericanos en España, ofreciendo entre otros datos, noticias científicas, bibliografía, directorios de investigadores y de centros. Estos contenidos se exportan de forma automática al portal europeo, de modo que constituye la aportación española al proyecto.

Las secciones de revistas de ambos portales de REDIAL cumplen por lo tanto con la función de identificar y difundir las publicaciones representativas de los estudios latinoamericanos. Se incluye un total de noventa y un títulos, de los cuáles solo diez representan publicaciones que ya no se editan. En la mayor parte de los casos se procede también al vaciado de los artículos de cada número, pero en el catálogo se incluyen también diecisiete boletines electrónicos de carácter periodístico o con datos de coyuntura económica y política. Sobre este tipo de publicaciones no se reflejan los datos de los artículos en el portal. De esta manera, en total hay sesenta y cuatro revistas consideradas como publicaciones académicas representativas de los estudios latinoamericanos en España, de las que sí se ofrece información bibliográfica de los artículos que publican.

En consecuencia, el número de revistas seleccionadas en los portales de REDIAL es sensiblemente más amplio que en ISOC y Latindex. Mientras en REDIAL se presentan ochenta y un títulos vivos y se ofrece información de los artículos en sesenta y cuatro casos, en ISOC y Latindex se consideran como especializadas en estudios latinoamericanos solamente cuarenta y una y la actualización de datos bibliográficos en ISOC se ha reducido a treinta y una. Esto se debe a la aplicación de un criterio más abierto en el caso de REDIAL, que afecta tanto a publicaciones que no superan el sistema de evaluación por parámetros formales de calidad editorial, como a otras que sí figuran en estos sistemas pero a las cuáles se les ha asignado otra clasificación temática. En general, todas las revistas consideradas en la categoría de estudios latinoamericanos, pueden a su vez pertenecer a otro ámbito temático, como literatura, historia, ciencias políticas, etc. Mientras que en los sistemas multidisciplinarios como ISOC o Latindex se puede optar por considerar publicaciones de esta índole entre los estudios regionales o bien dentro de las categorías disciplinarias, o en ambas; en el caso de los portales de REDIAL solo cabe incluirlas o dejarlas en el olvido. El problema radica en la existencia de publicaciones en las cuales no resulta fácil determinar si es apropiado considerarlas o no entre los estudios latinoamericanos. Estas dificultades serán analizadas en los apartados siguientes.

Diferencias de cobertura en las revistas españolas clasificadas en estudios latinoamericanos en ISOC, Latindex y portales de REDIAL

Entre las revistas españolas seleccionadas en los portales de REDIAL, se perciben claras diferencias en el grado de cobertura o especialización en los estudios latinoamericanos. No se trata de un conjunto homogéneo, sino que en numerosos casos se trata de publicaciones que incluyen también artículos de carácter teórico o sobre otras regiones geográficas.

Para este trabajo se han tomado en consideración los contenidos de las cincuenta y cinco publicaciones que se incluyen de forma actualizada con el

Tabla 2. Porcentaje de artículos sobre
América Latina en las revistas españolas
analizadas en los portales de REDIAL.

Contenido sobre América Latina	Número de revistas	%
100%	16	29%
80–99%	9	16%
60–80%	13	24%
40–60%	12	22%
Menos del 40%	5	9%
Total	**55**	**100%**

Fuente: Portal Americanismo.es; Base de datos ISOC 2010.

vaciado de los sumarios para los años 2008–2009. De las cuales, solo dieciséis dedican el 100 por ciento de sus artículos en este periodo a los temas latinoamericanos. Como puede verse en la tabla 2, en más de la mitad de los casos los estudios latinoamericanos suponen menos del 80 por ciento; y en cinco títulos se sitúan por debajo del 40 por ciento, llegando incluso al 17 por ciento.

Si para presentar una relación de publicaciones especializadas en estudios latinoamericanos se tuvieran en cuenta solamente aquellas que editan únicamente o casi exclusivamente artículos sobre esta región geográfica, la lista se limitaría a veinticinco títulos (el 45 por ciento de las analizadas). Sin embargo, hay varios argumentos para ampliar esta selección.

Por un lado, existen revistas que claramente se definen como iberoamericanas o hispanoamericanas, por su título o en su definición de objetivos, y que sin embargo también incluyen una cantidad importante de artículos sobre temas ibéricos. El ejemplo más representativo de este modelo es *Cuadernos Hispanoamericanos*, una publicación de la Agencia Española de Cooperación Internacional para el Desarrollo (AECID), la cual a pesar de que su título expresa una vocación claramente americanista, dedica a menudo su sección central a temas de cultura y literatura española. De los cincuenta y cinco casos analizados, en dos se incluye la palabra "hispánico," en una "latino" y en dieciocho "iberoamericano" dentro del título. Estos términos conllevan cierta ambigüedad debido a que pueden emplearse para referirse a los países americanos de habla española y portuguesa, o bien de manera más amplia para incluir también a los países ibéricos. En algunas de estas revistas los contenidos sobre América Latina son dominantes, pero no ocurre así en todas ellas. Por ejemplo *Cuadernos de Música Iberoamericana* es una publicación del Instituto Complutense de Estudios Musicales, cuyos contenidos sobre América Latina se limitan al 23 por ciento de los artículos publicados en la historia de la revista.

Por otro lado, hay otro grupo de publicaciones que dedica atención a América Latina de forma frecuente, pero únicamente en números monográficos concretos. Ejemplo de ello son *África América Latina Cuadernos, Monteagudo* o *Revista CIDOB d'Afers Internacionals*. Se trata de publicaciones que incluyen este continente entre sus líneas de interés prioritario, pero cuya práctica editorial responde a la preparación de temas que pueden estar referidos o no a lo latinoamericano. En estos casos, la presencia de artículos sobre la región es aleatoria e imprevisible.

Finalmente, también se constata la presencia de publicaciones que no se definen como iberoamericanas, pero que destacan por el alto número de artículos sobre América Latina. En la tabla 3 puede observarse la lista de las revistas españolas que aportan una mayor cantidad de documentos relativos a Latinoamérica en estos dos años (2008–2009). En este cálculo solamente se han tenido en cuenta los trabajos de investigación, no textos literarios, notas o reseñas. En los diez primeros títulos se encuentran varios ejemplos de títulos que quedarían al margen si se aplicaran criterios muy selectivos. Por un lado, *Cuadernos Hispanoamericanos*, *REICE* o *RIEE* son productos de carácter iberoamericano, más que latinoamericano. Por otra parte, surgen otros títulos

Tabla 3. Las 10 primeras revistas españolas por número de artículos sobre América Latina en el periodo septiembre de 2008.

Orden	Revista	Artículos Am. Lat.	Total artículos	% Am. Latina
1	Espéculo	243	507	48%
2	Cuadernos Hispanoamericanos	106	162	65%
3	Iberoamericana	88	103	85%
4	Scripta Nova	71	204	35%
5	Turydes	62	84	74%
6	REICE Revista Electrónica Iberoamericana sobre Calidad, Eficacia y Cambio en Educación	59	80	74%
7	Revista Española de Antropología Americana	54	56	96%
8	Revista de Indias	51	52	98%
9	Gazeta de Antropología	45	115	39%
10	RIEE Revista Iberoamericana de Evaluación Educativa	43	59	73%
10	Anuario de Estudios Americanos	43	44	98%

Fuente: Portal Americanismo.es; Base de datos ISOC 2010.

que no figuran clasificados en la categoría estudios latinoamericanos en ISOC o Latindex, como *Espéculo*, *Scripta Nova*, *Turydes* y *Gazeta de Antropología*.

Casos singulares de revistas electrónicas con contenidos sobre América Latina

En la lista de las cinco revistas españolas que aportaron mayor número de artículos al año sobre América Latina en el periodo 2008–2009 (tabla 3), destaca la presencia de dos títulos en los cuáles los documentos sobre esta región no llegan al 50 por ciento del total publicado en ellas en estos dos años.

En el primer lugar por su aportación se sitúa *Espéculo*, editada por la Facultad de Ciencias de la Información de la Universidad Complutense de Madrid (Departamento de Filología Española III).[10] Se define como una revista electrónica de estudios literarios. Su primer número se elaboró en noviembre de 1995, con únicamente cuatro artículos, ninguno concerniente a la literatura latinoamericana. En sus líneas de interés se menciona la literatura española y la literatura universal, no se cita la latinoamericana. El departamento que la edita tampoco está especializado en esta temática. En el consejo editorial únicamente hay miembros españoles. Y sin embargo en los últimos años se ha convertido, a diferencia, en la publicación española con mayor número de trabajos sobre América Latina.

En el cuarto lugar figura *Scripta Nova*, una publicación exclusivamente electrónica elaborada desde 1997 por la Universidad de Barcelona como parte de los contenidos alojados en el portal Geocrítica.[11] Se define como una revista de geografía y ciencias sociales. Por lo tanto, en su adscripción temática no hace referencia a los estudios latinoamericanos, aunque en su presentación manifiesta un interés por dirigirse "al público español e iberoamericano."[12] En este caso sí hay miembros latinoamericanos en su consejo de redacción: de Brasil, México, Chile, Perú y Colombia; acompañados de representantes de Argentina y Venezuela en el consejo asesor.

En ambos casos se trata de publicaciones que nacieron en los años noventa en formato electrónico. Su modelo editorial no es una copia de los procesos tradicionales, como ocurre en otras revistas que provienen de una extensa tra-dición en el medio impreso; sino que intenta aplicar un sistema menos apretado por las restricciones habituales de la lentitud y el coste de los envíos por correo postal. En estos títulos no existe una limitación en el número de artículos lo cual ha facilitado la inclusión de contribuciones de autores latinoamericanos, aunado a la facilidad que ofrece la difusión en acceso abierto por Internet. En la tabla 4 puede observarse como la aportación de los autores ligados a instituciones españolas se sitúa tan solo al rededor del 10 por ciento de los trabajos del tema latinoamericano en estas dos revistas. Por el contrario, en el periodo 2008–2009 un 85 por ciento de estos artículos procedieron de autores radicados en América.

Tabla 4. Aportación por países de afiliación institucional de
los autores en los trabajos sobre América Latina publicados en
Espéculo y *Scripta Nova* en el periodo septiembre 2008.

País de afiliación de los autores (lugar de trabajo)	Espéculo Art. sobre Am. Lat.	%	Scripta Nova Art. sobre Am. Lat.	%
España	20	9%	7	10%
Brasil	39	18%	37	52%
Argentina	47	21%	10	14%
México	22	10%	6	8%
Resto América Lat.	41	18%	8	11%
Estados Unidos	33	15%	0	0%
Europa	7	3%	5	7%
Otros	13	6%	0	0%
Total de artículos con datos de afiliación de autores	**222**	**100%**	**71**[13]	**100%**

Fuente: Portal Americanismo.es; Base de datos ISOC 2010.

La participación de los autores latinoamericanos y de otros países es también frecuente actualmente en las publicaciones más tradicionales del americanismo español. De este modo, por ejemplo, en los artículos del periodo 2008–2009, los autores españoles aportaron tan solo el 40 por ciento de las contribuciones publicadas en *Revista de Indias* y el 36 por ciento en *Anuario de Estudios Americanos*. Ambas revistas editadas por el CSIC desde la década de 1940 han representado durante muchos años la imagen del americanismo español, centrado en los temas históricos. Actualmente son revistas consideradas por los catálogos internacionales de citas que atraen a especialistas de todo el mundo.

Otros ejemplos de revistas españolas que se dedican parcialmente a los estudios latinoamericanos

A pesar de que la relación de publicaciones españolas recogidas en los portales de REDIAL resulta ya bastante amplia, existen otros ejemplos de revistas que no quedan reflejadas en dicha selección por tratarse de casos en los que la presencia de lo latinoamericano es menos visible. Se trata de títulos en los que hay una presencia continua de artículos sobre América Latina, pero que habitualmente quedan por debajo del 50 por ciento de las contribuciones totales.

En el noveno lugar de la lista de diez revistas españolas que aportaron mayor número de artículos al año sobre América Latina en el periodo

2008–2009 (tabla 3), se localiza una publicación que no está considerada entre los estudios latinoamericanos en ninguno de los sistemas presentados en este trabajo (ni ISOC, ni Latindex, ni REDIAL). Se trata de *Gazeta de Antropología*, editada por la Universidad de Granada. En el gráfico 1 puede observarse que en los últimos diez años la presencia de artículos sobre América Latina en esta publicación ha sido constante, si bien solamente ha superado el 50 por ciento de lo editado en el año en dos ocasiones (2005 y 2006). Este título no presenta un enfoque americanista ni en su denominación ni en su presentación y tanto en el consejo de redacción como en el consejo asesor no participan miembros latinoamericanos. Se trata de una revista que nació en formato impreso en 1991, sin embargo desde 1999 abandonó esta modalidad y se publica exclusivamente en forma electrónica, lo cuál ha podido ayudar a su mayor difusión para los autores de América Latina.

En los portales de REDIAL se incluyeron publicaciones como *Espéculo* y *Scripta Nova* con el argumento de que resultaban indispensables para caracterizar las publicaciones americanistas españolas por el alto número de artículos publicados anualmente sobre América Latina, lo que las situaba en los primeros lugares en cifras absolutas. Pero este criterio plantea serias dudas sobre dónde marcar la línea divisoria, que número o lugar en el *ranking* constituye el punto de inflexión para considerar o no que una publicación es representativa de los estudios latinoamericanos en España.

Al igual que en *Gazeta de Antropología* existen numerosos títulos que aportan una presencia constante de artículos americanistas, normalmente sin llegar al 50 por ciento de la edición anual. Como ocurre con la *Revista de Dialectología y Tradiciones Populares*, una de las revistas editadas desde el Centro de Ciencias Humanas y Sociales del CSIC en Madrid, en concreto por el Instituto de Lengua, Literatura y Antropología (ILLA). En el periodo

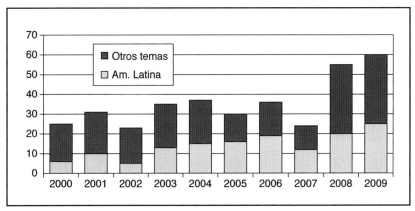

Gráfico 1. Evolución de los artículos sobre América Latina en *Gazeta de Antropología*, en el periodo septiembre 2000.
Fuente: Base de datos ISOC 2010.

2008–2009 publicó catorce artículos sobre América Latina, un 37 por ciento del total. En este caso más de la mitad eran artículos de autores españoles, y varios de ellos eran investigadores de la propia institución editora. Además la presencia de documentos sobre América Latina se ha mantenido en el tiempo, de forma continua desde 1993, con algunas ausencias pero con cierta frecuencia en años anteriores. Pero solamente en el año 2008 llegó a suponer el 50 por ciento de los artículos, como puede apreciarse en el gráfico 2.

La *Revista de Dialectología y Tradiciones Populares*, fundada en 1944, es la más veterana de las publicaciones españolas especializadas en antropología y folklore. Mantiene la edición impresa pero cuenta también con una versión electrónica de acceso abierto. En su definición de temática y alcance no determina ninguna línea de interés por lo iberoamericano. Sin embargo el centro editor, el ILLA, cuenta con un grupo de investigación de antropología comparada de España y América, cuyos integrantes publican habitualmente en esta revista, o pueden proponer a otros colegas que envíen sus contribuciones. Por ello, puede concluirse que no se trata de una publicación de vocación americanista, pero que mantiene una presencia continua de los temas latinoamericanos como reflejo del peso del americanismo dentro de la antropología española y como parte de las líneas de trabajo de la institución editora.

Ejemplos similares pueden encontrarse en otras publicaciones de esta disciplina, como la *Revista de Antropología Experimental*, editada por la Universidad de Jaén (gráfico 3). Se trata nuevamente de una publicación electrónica.

Un fenómeno similar puede verse en publicaciones de investigación histórica gestionadas desde departamentos universitarios que cuentan con un área de historia de América.[14] Un ejemplo es la revista *Trocadero*, del Departamento de Historia Moderna, Contemporánea, de América y del Arte de la Universidad

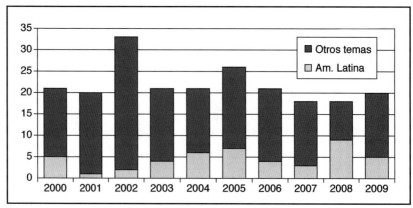

Gráfico 2. Evolución de los artículos sobre América Latina en *Revista de Dialectología y Tradiciones Populares*, en el periodo septiembre 2000.
Fuente: Base de datos ISOC 2010.

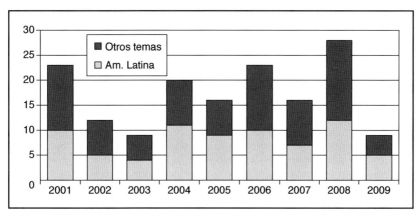

Gráfico 3. Evolución de los artículos sobre América Latina en *Revista de Antropología Experimental*, en el periodo septiembre 2001.
Fuente: Base de datos 2010.

de Cádiz. La presencia de artículos sobre América Latina es continua y se sitúa habitualmente en una tercera parte de la publicación. Sin embargo no se puede establecer una pauta fija de comportamiento. La publicación *Investigaciones Históricas*, del Departamento de Historia Moderna, Contemporánea y de América de la Universidad de Valladolid, no incluye ningún trabajo sobre América Latina desde el año 2000. Por lo tanto, no es posible concluir *a priori* que toda revista de los departamentos con área de historia de América constituya una publicación americanista.

Por el contrario, sí es frecuente la inclusión de artículos sobre América Latina en otras publicaciones del Instituto de Historia, en el Centro de Ciencias Humanas y Sociales del CSIC, a pesar de no pertenecer a departamentos específicos de historia de América. Tanto la revista *Asclepio* de historia de la medicina y de la ciencia, como *Hispania Sacra*, de historia de la iglesia, dedicaron a Latinoamérica un 20 por ciento de sus contenidos editados en el periodo 2000–2009. En estos casos influye la tradición de estas publicaciones y la importancia de las relaciones científicas internacionales, que en estas disciplinas se dirigen con mucha frecuencia hacia el área iberoamericana.

Conclusiones

En este trabajo se han tomado en cuenta los sistemas de categorización de revistas españolas de la base de datos ISOC del CSIC, la red iberoamericana Latindex y los portales de la asociación europea REDIAL. Los resultados de la comparación muestran algunas diferencias entre ellos, a pesar de que los datos sobre España en estos tres sistemas proceden de la misma institución, el Centro de Ciencias Humanas y Sociales del CSIC. Hay coincidencia en las cifras sobre los títulos especializados en estudios latinoamericanos entre ISOC y Latindex, sin embargo difieren en la presentación de un núcleo de revistas de mayor calidad. En ambos casos se consideran cuarenta y un revistas vigentes, pero Latindex incluye veintitrés en su catálogo, mientras que el Directorio de Revistas Españolas de Ciencias Sociales y Humanas de la base de datos ISOC muestra treinta y una en las categorías A, B o C. Este conjunto define el núcleo básico con el cual en este momento se actualizan las referencias en la subbase de datos ISOC-América Latina.

Por el contrario, en los portales de REDIAL se presentan ochenta y un títulos vivos y se ofrece información de los artículos en sesenta y cuatro casos. En este sistema de información, constituido por un portal de marco español y otro europeo que comparten los mismos datos, se aplica un criterio de selección más abierto, para poder abarcar un panorama suficientemente representativo de la presencia de los estudios latinoamericanos en las publicaciones españolas.

Existen revistas claramente especializadas que se circunscriben exclusivamente a las investigaciones sobre esta región geográfica. Si se limitara la selección a las publicaciones con estas características, quedarían tan solo veinticinco títulos. Por lo tanto, no solo en los portales de REDIAL, también en Latindex e ISOC se aplican filtros más abiertos. Pero los criterios empleados plantean dudas en cuanto a los casos de inclusión de revistas con contenido habitual pero no exclusivo sobre América Latina:

a) Se pueden considerar en la adscripción temática a los estudios latinoamericanos aquellas publicaciones que se definen como iberoamericanas, latinas o hispánicas. Así como aquellas que citan expresamente a América Latina entre sus áreas de interés, aunque no de forma exclusiva. Sin embargo, la publicación o no de un número suficiente de artículos sobre Latinoamérica resulta variable e imprevisible, en especial en las revistas que suelen abordar temas concretos en la modalidad de números monográficos.

b) Se pueden obtener en la base ISOC datos sobre publicaciones que aportan una gran cantidad de artículos anuales relativos a América Latina, aunque habitualmente suponen menos del 50 por ciento de los editados por estas revistas en el año. Aunque no se definan como títulos especializados en estudios latinoamericanos, resultan indispensables para caracterizar la presencia de estas investigaciones en España, debido a que en algunos casos superan en número de artículos a las publicaciones específicas. Sin embargo, la presencia o no de artículos sobre América Latina resulta igualmente imprevisible y a menudo depende de la libre aportación de los autores latinoamericanos.

En ambas modalidades, resulta justificada su inclusión en una relación de revistas españolas de estudios latinoamericanos, aunque no resulta fácil fijar un criterio uniforme sobre su inclusión, ya que los datos sobre la cantidad de artículos publicados pueden variar notablemente de un año a otro.

Varias de las revistas presentadas son publicaciones electrónicas. Este factor está siendo decisivo a la hora de atraer el interés de los autores latinoamericanos para publicar sus trabajos en las revistas españolas. No puede considerarse que sea un factor único, puesto que este fenómeno no afecta por igual a todas las revistas españolas con versión electrónica de acceso abierto. Para justificar que algunas publicaciones se signifiquen en la presencia creciente de contenidos latinoamericanos, se debe tener en cuenta igualmente la existencia de redes de colaboración que a menudo no se muestran con claridad.

En cualquier caso, los estudios latinoamericanos se encuentran muy dispersos en las publicaciones españolas de las diferentes disciplinas de ciencias sociales y humanas, y se nutren cada vez más de la aportación de investigadores relacionados a instituciones no españolas. El núcleo central de revistas especializadas define una corriente principal de expresión de los estudios americanistas, pero no puede obviarse ni dejarse al margen la existencia de otras publicaciones no específicas cuya aportación es importante ya sea por el número total de artículos anuales sobre América Latina o bien por su peso específico dentro de la publicación.

NOTAS

1. Román y Rojo y Toledo, "¿Tienen las revistas españolas?" 425.

2. Yunta. "Situación de las publicaciones españolas."

3. Las bases de datos del CSIC se distribuyen en la página web: http://bddoc.csic.es:8085/. El acceso precisa suscripción. Existe además una versión reducida que solo permite la consulta de la información extraída de los sumarios de las revistas, a la que se accede en la web http://bddoc.csic.es:8080/.

4. http://hdl.handle.net/10261/41567.

5. La dirección de consulta de Latindex está en la página web http://www.latindex.unam.mx/. En esta web se define como "producto de la cooperación de una red de instituciones que funcionan de manera coordinada para reunir y diseminar información bibliográfica sobre las publicaciones científicas seriadas producidas en la región."

6. El Grupo EPUC se constituyó en 1996 en el Centro de Información y Documentación Científica (CINDOC). Actualmente se integra en el Instituto de Estudios Documentales sobre Ciencia y Tecnología (IEDCYT) del Centro de Ciencias Humanas y Sociales del CSIC. Su página web es: http://humanidades.cchs.csic.es/cchs/epuc/index.php.

7. Román y Alcain, "Una apuesta por la calidad."

8. Estas valoraciones corresponden a los datos de 2006. En 2010 se está procediendo a una nueva encuesta para poder presentar una nueva actualización de los resultados.

9. http://www.americanismo.es y http://www.red-redial.net.

10. http://www.ucm.es/info/especulo/.

11. http://www.ub.es/geocrit/nova.htm.

12. Capel, "Presentación."

13. En este caso el total de artículos no se corresponde con la suma aritmética de los datos, pues existen 2 artículos en colaboración de varios autores en los que se suman lugares de trabajo de diferentes países.

14. La Historia de América es la única especialidad relacionada directamente con los Estudios Latinoamericanos que aparece contemplada en España en la regulación de áreas del conocimiento de la ANECA (Agencia Nacional de Evaluación de la Calidad y Acreditación). Sin embargo solo constituye un departamento exclusivo en la Universidad Complutense de Madrid y en la Universidad de Sevilla. En las restantes figura como área integrada en un departamento más amplio.

BIBLIOGRAFÍA

Capel, Horacio. "Presentación." *Scripta Nova. Revista Electrónica de Geografía y Ciencias Sociales*. http://www.ub.edu/geocrit/sn-pres.htm.

Román, Adelaida Román, Angela Sorli Rojo y Elea Giménez Toledo. "¿Tienen las revistas españolas de estudios latinoamericanos los niveles de internacionalización esperables, dado su ámbito de especialización?" *Anuario Americanista Europea* no.4–5 (2006–2007): 425–40. http://www.red-redial.net/revista/anuario-americanista-europeo/article/viewFile/96/81.

Román, Adelaida Román y María Dolores Alcain. "Una apuesta por la calidad en la selección de las revistas españolas." *Clip Boletín de la SEDIC*, no. 44 (2006). http://www.sedic.es/p_boletinclip44_confirma.asp.

Yunta, Luis Rodríguez. "Situación de las publicaciones españolas sobre Estudios Latinoamericanos." Presentado en el LIV Encuentro SALALM: Migrations and Connections: Latin America and Europe in the Modern World, Berlin, Alemania, julio 2009.

APÉNDICE:

RELACIÓN DE REVISTAS ANALIZADAS EN EL TRABAJO

Revistas presentes en el Directorio de Revistas Españolas de Ciencias Sociales y Humanas de la base de datos ISOC, clasificadas en el área temática América Latina

Revistas en categoría A (muy alta):
– *Anuario de Estudios Americanos*. 0210–5810 (1944–).
– *Revista Complutense de Historia de América*. 1132–8312 (1991–).
– *Revista de Indias*. 0034–8341 (1940–).

Revistas en categoría B (alta):
– *Anales de Literatura Hispanoamericana*. 0210–4547 (1972–).
– *Revista Española de Antropología Americana*. 0556–6533 (1952–).

Revistas en categoría C (normal):
- *A-mérika*. 1989–6875 (2009–).
- *América Latina Hoy: Revista de Ciencias Sociales*. 1130–2887 (1991–).
- *América sin Nombre*. 1577–3442 (1999–).
- *Anales: Museo de América*. 1133–8741 (1993–).
- *Anuario Americanista Europeo*. 1729–9004 (2003–).
- *Araucaria: Revista Iberoamericana de Filosofía, Política y Humanidades*. 1575–6823 (1999–).
- *Arqueología Iberoamericana*. 1989–4104 (2009–).
- *Boletín Americanista*. 0520–4100 (1959–).
- *Cuadernos de Música Iberoamericana*. 1136–5536 (1996–).
- *Cuadernos Hispanoamericanos*. 0011–250X (1948–).
- *Debate y Perspectivas: Cuadernos de Historia y Ciencias Sociales*. 1567–1261 (2000–2006).
- *Delos: Desarrollo Local Sostenible*. 1988–5245 (2007–).
- *Estudios de Historia Social y Económica de América*. 0214–2236 (1985–1998).
- *Estudios Económicos de Desarrollo Internacional*. 1578–4479 (2001–).
- *HIB: Revista de Historia Iberoamericana*. 1989–2616 (2008–).
- *Iberoamericana: América Latina España Portugal*. 1577–3388 (2001–).
- *Instituciones y Desarrollo*. 1560–5264 (1998–2006).
- *Mayab*. 1130–6157 (1985–).
- *Naveg@merica*. 1989–211X (2008–).
- *Observatorio Iberoamericano del Desarrollo Local y la Economía Social, OIDLES*. 1988–2483 (2007–).
- *Pensamiento Iberoamericano*. 0212–0208 (1982–).
- *Quorum: Revista de Pensamiento Iberoamericano*. 1575–4227 (2000–).
- *Revista de Estudios Colombinos*. 1699–3926 (2005–).
- *Revista Electrónica Iberoamericana*. 1988–0618 (2007–).
- *Revista Iberoamericana de Autogestión y Acción Comunal*. 0212–7687 (1983–).
- *RIED: Revista Iberoamericana de Educación a Distancia*. 1138–2783 (1998–).
- *Síntesis: Revista Documental de Ciencias Sociales Iberoamericanas*. 0213–7577 (1987–2000).
- *Tecsistecatl: Revista Electrónica de Ciencias Sociales*. 1886–8452 (2007–).
- *Tiempos de América: Revista de Historia, Cultura y Territorio*. 1138–1310 (1997–).
- *UniverSOS*. 1698–6083 (2004–).

Sin categorizar:
- *África América Latina Cuadernos*. 1130–2569 (1990–).
- *Arrabal*. 1138–7459 (1998–).
- *Baluarte: Estudios Gaditano-Cubanos*. 1135–7983 (1994–2002).
- *Cádiz e Iberoamérica*. 1130–0302 (1983–1992).

- *Cuadernos de Arte Colonial.* 0213–6717 (1986–1992).
- *Cuadernos Prehispánicos.* 0302–6728 (1973–1999).
- *Encuentro de la Cultura Cubana.* 1136–6389 (1996–).
- *Guaraguao: Revista de Cultura Latinoamericana.* 1137–2354 (1996–).
- *Historiografía y Bibliografía Americanistas.* 0439–2477 (1954–1987).
- *Illes i Imperis.* 1575–0698 (1998–).
- *Indigenismo.* 0213–2907 (1982–1990).
- *Mar Oceana.* 1134–7627 (1994–).
- *Quaderns d'Amèrica (Separata de l'Avenç).* 1130–5169 (1987–1992).
- *Quinto Centenario.* 0211–6111 (1981–1990).
- *Rábida.* 1130–5088 (1985–).
- *Redial: Revista Europea de Información y Documentación sobre América Latina.* 1019–8563 (1992–1998).
- *Revista da Comisión Galega do Quinto Centenario.* (1989–1990).
- *Situación Latinoamericana.* 1130–9466 (1991–1999).
- *Suplemento de Anuario de Estudios Americanos. Sección Historiografía y Bibliografía Americanista.* 0214–2252 (1987–1993).
- *Temas Americanistas.* 0212–4408 (1982–).
- *Travesías: Política, Cultura y Sociedad en Iberoamérica.* 1136–8780 (1996).
- *Tribuna Americana: Revista de Reflexión Política.* 1696–4365 (2003–2006).

Revistas recogidas en los portales de REDIAL, pero clasificadas en otras áreas en ISOC, no como estudios latinoamericanos

Revistas en categoría A (muy alta):
- *Revista de Historia Económica: Journal of Iberian and Latin American Economic History.* 0212–6109 (1983–).
- *Scripta Nova: Revista Electrónica de Geografía y Ciencias Sociales.* 1138–9788 (1997–).

Revistas en categoría B (alta):
- *Anuario de Lingüística Hispánica.* 0213–053X (1985–).

Revistas en categoría C (normal):
- *AIBR: Revista de Antropología Iberoamericana.* 1695–9752 (2000–).
- *Anuario de Estudios Atlánticos.* 0570–4065 (1955–).
- *Anuario Iberoamericano de Justicia Constitucional.* 1138–4824 (1997–).
- *Espéculo: Revista de Estudios Literarios.* 1139–3637 (1995–).
- *Monteagudo: Revista de Literatura Española, Hispanoamericana y Teoría de la Literatura.* 0580–6712 (1953–).
- *REICE: Revista Electrónica Iberoamericana de Calidad, Eficacia y Cambio en Educación.* 1696–4713 (2003–).

– *Revista CIDOB d'Afers Internacionals.* 1133–6595 (1985–).
– *Revista de Hispanismo Filosófico.* 1136–8071 (1996–).
– *Revista Española de Desarrollo y Cooperación.* 1137–8875 (1997–).
– *Revista Iberoamericana de Educación.* 1022–6508 (1993–).
– *Revista Latina de Comunicación Social* 1138–5820 (1998–).
– *Turydes: Revista de Investigación en Turismo y Desarrollo Local.* 1988–5261 (2007–).

Publicaciones recogidas en los portales de REDIAL, y no presentes en el directorio de la base ISOC

– *Americaeconomica* (1999–).
– *Anuario Iberoamericano* (1989–).
– *ARI: Análisis del Real Instituto.* 1696–3466 (2003–).
– *Boletín Brasil* (2004–).
– *Boletín del Real Instituto Elcano.* 1696–3326 (2002–).
– *Boletín Elites Parlamentarias Latinoamericanas* (2005–).
– *Cuadernos de América sin Nombre* (2000–).
– *Cuadernos Escénicos.* 1577–7669 (1999–2003).
– *Cuba Económica* (1999–).
– *Datamex: Análisis de Coyuntura Mensual sobre México.* 1135–8130 (2001–).
– *DHIAL: Desarrollo Humano e Institucional para América Latina.* 1577–5232 (2000–2006).
– *Documentos CIDOB: América Latina.* 1697–7688 (2004–).
– *Documentos de Trabajo IELAT–IAES.* (2009–).
– *Documentos de Trabajo IELAT.* (2008–).
– *Esbozos: Revista de Filosofía Política y Ayuda al Desarrollo.* (2009–).
– *Estudios Afroamericanos Virtual.* 1697–4255 (2004–2005).
– *Ética y Gobernabilidad.* (2003–2006).
– *Gobernanza: Revista Internacional para el Desarrollo Humano.* 1697–5669 (2004–2006).
– *La Estafeta del Viento: Revista de Poesía de la Casa de América.* 1579–5861 (2002–2006).
– *Mercosur.* (1995–).
– *Observatorio de la Economía Latinoamericana.* 1696–8352 (2002–).
– *Ojos de Papel.* (1999–).
– *Papeles de Trabajo: América Latina Siglo XXI.* 1989–1377 (2008–).
– *Pensar Iberoamérica: Revista de Cultura.* 1683–3783 (2002–2006).
– *Revibec: Revista Iberoamericana de Economía Ecológica.* 1390–2776 (2004–).
– *Revista de las Américas: Historia y Presente.* 1696–1900 (2003).
– *Revista Galega de Cooperación Científica Iberoamericana.* 1134–9050 (1994–2005).
– *Revista Global Hoy.* (2003–).

– *Revista Hispano Cubana*. 1139–0883 (1998–).
– *Revista Iberoamericana de Ciencia, Tecnología y Sociedad*. 1850–0013 (2003–).
– *Revista Internacional de Lingüística Iberoamericana*. 1579–9425 (2003–).
– *Revista Mural: Casa de América*. 1578–0325 (2004–2006).
– *RIEE: Revista Iberoamericana de Evaluación Educativa*. 1989–0397 (2008–).
– *Voxlocalis*. (2006–).

Otras revistas citadas en el trabajo, que no figuran en los portales de REDIAL, pero mantienen una aportación constante a los estudios americanistas y cuyos artículos sobre esta región figuran en la subbase ISOC-América Latina

– *Asclepio: Revista de Historia de la Medicina y de la Ciencia*. 0210–4466 (1964–).
– *Gazeta de Antropología*. 0214–7564 (1991–).
– *Hispania Sacra*. 0018–215X (1948–).
– *Revista de Antropología Experimental*. 1578–4282 (2001–).
– *Revista de Dialectología y Tradiciones Populares*. 0034–7981 (1944–).
– *Trocadero: Revista de Historia Moderna y Contemporánea*. 0214–4212 (1989–).

12. La contribución del CLADES de la CEPAL al desarrollo de los sistemas de información en América Latina

Micaela Chávez Villa
Víctor J. Cid Carmona

Este trabajo tiene como objetivo hacer una reseña sobre las distintas acciones que el Centro Latinoamericano de Documentación Económica y Social (CLADES), dependiente de la Secretaría Ejecutiva de la Comisión Económica para América Latina (CEPAL), llevó a cabo ante los cambios que se estaban produciendo en el ámbito económico al inicio de la década de los setenta. Entre estos cambios se señalaba como el más significativo "la identificación de la información como elemento básico en la planificación del desarrollo y la consecuente necesidad de crear infraestructuras de información nacionales, regionales o internacionales capaces de hacer expedito el flujo de información, desde su generación hasta su utilización eficaz."[1]

A manera de introducción se esboza brevemente el origen de la CEPAL y sus contribuciones más importantes al desarrollo de la región.

Comisión Económica Para América Latina

Origen

En 1947 Hernán Santa Cruz, representante del gobierno chileno entregó oficialmente al Secretario General de las Naciones Unidas un proyecto de resolución concerniente a la creación de la CEPAL. Este proyecto estaba fundamentado en la idea de que "América Latina había entrado en una grave crisis originada en el esfuerzo económico realizado para defender la causa de las Naciones Unidas en la guerra y en las perturbaciones que ésta había causado a la economía mundial; y en que era necesario desarrollar la industria de los países de América Latina y utilizar al máximo sus enormes recursos naturales para elevar el nivel de vida de sus habitantes, ayudar a resolver los problemas económicos de otros continentes, lograr un mejor equilibrio del edificio económico mundial e intensificar el comercio internacional."[2]

Después de un largo proceso de debate, en el segundo período de sesiones de la Asamblea General, la Comisión Económica y Financiera conformada por cincuenta y cinco países, integró en su orden del día el estudio del informe anual que el Consejo Económico y Social presentó a la Asamblea sobre sus actividades, dentro del proceso de análisis en el cual los "delegados de todas las naciones económicamente débiles hablaron a favor de la necesidad de que las Naciones Unidas cooperaran en forma activa con los gobiernos en sus políticas de desarrollo económico-social, en particular a través de organismos regionales como los que ya existían para Europa y para el Asia y Lejano Oriente."[3]

La iniciativa de crear la Comisión Económica para Oriente Medio incluyó dos consideraciones que se referían a la propuesta de creación de la Comisión para América Latina. Se nombró un comité ad hoc para analizar la situación y preparar el proyecto de resolución 106 (VI) que fue aprobado el 25 de enero de 1948 con trece votos a favor, cero en contra y cuatro abstenciones, que correspondieron a Bielorrusia, Canadá, Estados Unidos y la Unión Soviética.[4]

Objetivos

La CEPAL es una de las cinco comisiones regionales de las Naciones Unidas (véase figura 1) con sede en Santiago de Chile. Fue fundada para contribuir al desarrollo económico de América Latina, coordinar las acciones encaminadas a su promoción y reforzar las relaciones económicas de los

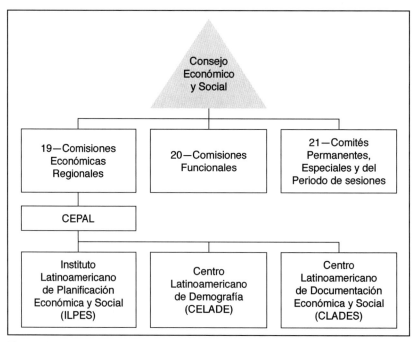

Figura 1. Estructura de la CEPAL (1971)
Fuente: Naciones Unidas, ABC de las Naciones Unidas, (Nueva York: Oficina de información Pública, 1971).

países entre sí así como con las demás naciones del mundo. Posteriormente su labor se amplió a los países del Caribe y se incorporó el objetivo de promover el desarrollo social.

La CEPAL tiene dos sedes subregionales, una para la subregión de América Central, ubicada en México, D.F. y la otra para la subregión del Caribe, situada en Puerto España, las cuales se establecieron en junio de 1951 y en diciembre de 1966, respectivamente. Además, tiene oficinas nacionales en Buenos Aires, Brasilia, Montevideo y Bogotá, así como una oficina de enlace en Washington, D.C.[5]

Sistema

El sistema de la CEPAL está comprendido por la propia Comisión, el Instituto Latinoamericano de Planificación Económica y Social (ILPES), el Centro Latinoamericano de Demografía (CELADE) y el Centro Latino-americano de Documentación Económica y Social (CLADES).[6]

El proyecto de información para el desarrollo

Desde sus inicios los especialistas de la CEPAL advirtieron la falta de información para la planeación y el desarrollo en los países de la región. Una de sus primeras acciones fue la compilación de información estadística que fue integrada en el Estudio Económico de América Latina el cual ha venido publicándose desde 1948.

Sin embargo era necesario diseñar las estrategias que aseguraran cumplir con la necesidad de tener infraestructuras de información a nivel nacional, regional e internacional, capaces de manejar el flujo de información desde su generación hasta las formas más eficientes de su utilización.

En 1969 el Gobierno de Holanda otorgó a la CEPAL el financiamiento para la creación de un centro de documentación económica y social, el cual cooperaría con el trabajo del ILPES en la investigación y análisis para atender las necesidades de los gobiernos de la región y establecería los medios para permitir el intercambio de información y la cooperación entre los países de América Latina.[7]

En 1970 se reunieron en la sede de la CEPAL en Santiago, Chile, docu-mentalistas, analistas y programadores de sistemas, oficiales del gobierno y agencias especializadas, economistas, sociólogos y otros usuarios de la documentación para definir las bases teóricas y funcionales sobre las cuales debería operar dicho centro, con el objetivo de resolver los problemas básicos de información de la región.

En atención a las conclusiones y recomendaciones de la reunión, y de acuerdo con el estudio de otros documentos relacionados, fue aprobada la Resolución 303, con fecha 6 de junio de 1971, en la que se destaca la "necesi-dad de que los países de América Latina posean modernos sistemas nacionales de información económica, social, científica, estadística y tecnológica."[8]

El Centro Latinoamericano de Documentación Económica y Social (CLADES)

De acuerdo con lo anterior, la creación del Centro Latinoamericano de Documentación Económica y Social (CLADES) surgió como respuesta a la "identificación de la información como elemento básico en la planificación del desarrollo y la consecuente necesidad de crear infraestructuras de información nacionales, regionales o internacionales capaces de hacer expedito el flujo de información, desde su generación, hasta su utilización más eficaz."[9]

Para cumplir lo indicado en la resolución 303, se realizó en septiembre de 1971 una reunión para discutir sobre técnicas modernas de documentación, la cual tuvo como resultado las siguientes recomendaciones:

I. Definir principios comunes para la normativización de tareas de documentación e información, promoviendo la creación de redes y sistemas aptos para el intercambio eficiente y efectivo en el ámbito de la información socioeconómica

II. Adoptar medidas jurídico-administrativas para asegurar la conservación y protección de los acervos documentales dispersos en instituciones públicas y privadas

III. Adecuar normas y técnicas compatibles para la recuperación de la información y documentación

IV. Integrar lenguajes documentales a través de la creación de un sistema de referencia terminológica uniforme

V. Coordinar esfuerzos con organismos nacionales e internacionales, de carácter público o privado, para la implementación de un plan de capacitación y formación de recursos humanos especializados, a través de talleres, cursos y seminarios, destinados al funcionamiento de redes nacionales y regionales de información y documentación[10]

Objetivos

Objetivo general de desarrollo:

I. Contribuir al desarrollo de América Latina y el Caribe mediante el apoyo a los países de la región por medio de la sistematización de sus recursos de información para el desarrollo económico y social

Objetivos específicos:

I. Fortalecer la capacidad de las instituciones nacionales de América Latina y el Caribe para la creación y operación de unidades y sistemas de manejo del recurso información

II. Facilitar la toma de decisiones sobre políticas nacionales de desarrollo económico y social, mediante la creación de mecanismos para permitir un fácil acceso a la información para el desarrollo por parte de planificadores, investigadores e instituciones públicas y privadas

III. Impulsar la concentración de actividades en información entre instituciones nacionales, regionales e internacionales que estuvieran operando en América Latina y el Caribe[11]

Rol y funciones

A partir de su fundación, corresponde al CLADES el rol de promotor de la interacción entre:

I. Las instituciones nacionales de investigación, estudio, planificación, coordinación, fomento, etc., generadoras de información

II. Las unidades de información nacionales que controlan, procesan y difunden información

III. Las redes y sistemas de información nacionales, regionales e internacionales sectoriales por disciplina o por misión

IV. Los usuarios de información, personas e instituciones[12]

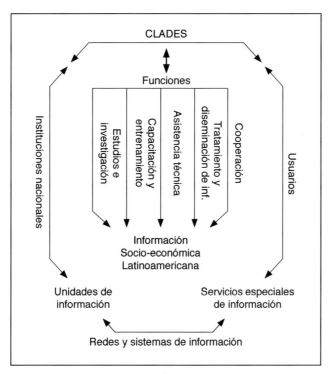

Fig. 2. Rol y funciones del CLADES[13]
Fuente: CLADES: Su rol y funciones 1977.

Las cinco funciones principales del CLADES se definieron a partir de la interacción con la región, con el objeto de dar respuesta a las necesidades detectadas y manifestadas por los países de la región....

I. Estudios e investigación

Se realizaron estudios e investigaciones sobre los siguientes asuntos:

a. Estudios de usuarios y sus necesidades

b. Estudios de instrumentos normalizados que posibiliten la compatibilización e interconexión de sistemas de información

c. Lenguajes de indización

d. Programas computacionales

e. Telecomunicaciones usadas en sistemas de información

f. Nuevas formas de almacenamiento y tratamiento de información[14]

II. Capacitación y entrenamiento

Basado en el conocimiento y experiencia obtenidos del en el desarrollo de sus programas de trabajo, dedicaron sus esfuerzos para la:

a. Formulación de metodologías de diagnóstico

b. Colaboración para la elección y aplicación de técnicas documentarias

c. Capacitación de recursos humanos para sistemas y servicios de documentación

d. Supervisión de montaje y puesta en marcha de sistemas de información

e. Capacitación para la aplicación e incorporación de nuevas tecnologías en el proceso de toma de decisiones

Por su parte, los solicitantes se hacían cargo de:

a. Preparar datos para elaborar y evaluar el diagnóstico

b. Definir las soluciones propuestas para el montaje, operación y control del sistema de información[15]

III. Asistencia técnica

Su propósito consistía en:

a. Apoyar a los países en el tratamiento de su información bibliográfica, económica y social

   b. Facilitar la toma de decisiones con respecto a las políticas nacionales de desarrollo económico y social, mediante la creación de mecanismos facilitadores de acceso a la información concerniente a planificadores, investigadores e instituciones públicas y privadas

Apoyaron técnicamente en los siguientes aspectos:

   a. Diagnóstico

   b. Diseño e implementación de centros y sistemas de información

   c. Normativización y compatibilización de sistemas

   d. Formatos y programas para procesamiento de datos

   e. Terminología para tratamiento de la información[16]

IV. Tratamiento y difusión de información

Los diagnósticos sobre el manejo de la información en América Latina demostraron que estaba insuficientemente organizada y por lo tanto, resultaba difícil acceder a ella.

Con respecto a lo anterior, se dedicaron esfuerzos a la preparación de instrumentos normativos para el tratamiento de la información, con el objeto de lograr la normativización de los sistemas de información a nivel nacional, regional e internacional, con miras a su posterior interconexión en una red.

Las acciones encaminadas a dicho propósito consistieron en:

   a. Elaborar normas, reglas, métodos, principios rectores y otros instrumentos para el tratamiento y transferencia de información así como para la creación de sistemas de información compatibles

   b. Estimular a los países de la región, individual y colectivamente, para crear sus propias bases de datos y acreditar las existentes a nivel internacional, con el objetivo de intensificar el intercambio y la circulación de información, aplicando nuevas tecnologías

   c. Proceder al intercambio y circulación de información, a la cooperación regional e internacional entre los estados miembros y con otros organismos del sistema de Naciones Unidas[17]

V. Cooperación

Su propósito consistía en fomentar y estimular la interacción entre instituciones, centros, redes y sistemas de información para el desarrollo de la región.

El CLADES apoyó las actividades relacionadas con el intercambio de información y los esfuerzos para la creación de redes y sistemas informativos nacionales y regionales, además de fortalecer los existentes. Coordinó las acciones para nivelar las tecnologías y los conocimientos de los recursos humanos involucrados en los procesos de intercambio de información.[18]

La información/documentación en América Latina

Basado en los diagnósticos de la CEPAL sobre los procesos de desarrollo económico y social de los países de la región, el CLADES consideró la situación de la información en la región en forma global, independientemente de las características particulares de ella en cada país.

A partir de lo anterior, el CLADES identificó siete áreas-problemas comunes en todos los países que afectaban en diversa medida los procesos de transferencia de información, a saber:

I. Ausencia de un diagnóstico completo de las infraestructuras de información en el campo económico y social

II. Obstáculos políticos y técnicos que perjudicaban la constitución de redes de intercambio de información

III. Duplicidad de servicios de información

IV. Deficiencias de vinculación entre los especialistas de información y los usuarios.

V. Deficiencias en la comunicación entre los especialistas de información

VI. Ausencia de herramientas y técnicas de documentación adecuadas a las necesidades y recursos de la región

VII. Carencia de metodologías realistas para el diseño e implementación de sistemas de información[19]

Los fundamentos de la estrategia de información del CLADES se basaron en tres enfoques de la problemática de la información:

I. La organización de la información—responde a dos esquemas conceptuales: el vertical o disciplinario y el horizontal o misionario (ciencias interdisciplinarias: salud, educación, medio ambiente, etc.)

II. El usuario de información para el desarrollo—se define al usuario como uno de los principales componentes

III. La desinformación—definida "como una situación en la que el sujeto-usuario y el objeto-información no se encuentran en la relación deseada"[20]

Principales acciones del CLADES y sus productos

Inventario de unidades de Información

En 1975 fue iniciado un proyecto con el fin de tener un inventario de unidades de información socioeconómica en América Latina y el Caribe en el que participaron veintidós países de la región.

Los principales resultados de dicho inventario fueron:[21]

I. El diagnóstico de las posibilidades y deficiencias de la infraestructura de información en el campo socio-económico a nivel regional

II. La determinación de las posibilidades y limitaciones en la infraestructura de información de cada país

III. El establecimiento de políticas de información regional y nacional a partir de los resultados de los diagnósticos previos

Entre los productos del inventario se cuentan los siguientes:[22]

I. La creación de una base de datos en CLADES con la información recopilada, organizada según los sistemas ISIS y SPSS

II. La impartición de seminarios de diagnóstico con las autoridades de cada país para discutir el informe de diagnóstico presentado por el CLADES y para redactar las recomendaciones enfocadas a orientar y promover el cambio

III. La transferencia de las metodologías aplicadas en la realización del proyecto y en el análisis de datos, mediante la capacitación de profesionales designados por los Gobiernos, con el fin de que fueran aplicadas en otros inventarios nacionales

IV. La entrega de estudios especiales sobre infraestructuras de información de algunos de los países de la región

Las publicaciones emanadas del proyecto fueron:

I. El directorio nacional de unidades de información para cada uno de los países participantes

II. El directorio regional

III. Informe sobre la infraestructura de información para el desarrollo en países seleccionados

IV. Informe de diagnóstico regional sobre infraestructura de información económica y social en América Latina y El Caribe

Sistema de Información para la Planificación (INFOPLAN)

Los antecedentes del proyecto se sitúan en 1977. Durante la Primera Conferencia de Ministros y Jefes de Planificación de América Latina y

El Caribe, en la cual se acordó la creación del Sistema de Cooperación y Coordinación entre Organismos de Planificación de América Latina, con el fin de promover el intercambio de experiencias nacionales en materia de planificación económica y social, además de fortalecer la cooperación. Se designó al Instituto Latinoamericano de Planificación (ILPES) como Secretaría Técnica, con el propósito de brindar apoyo a los gobiernos para el cumplimiento de los objetivos del proyecto.[23]

Los objetivos del proyecto fueron:[24]

Generales:

I. Contribuir al proceso de planificación del desarrollo económico y social de los países de América Latina y el Caribe mediante el control, análisis y difusión de la información documental producida por organismos relacionados con la planificación

II. Apoyar los programas del ILPES con un servicio de información sobre las experiencias de planificación en América Latina y el Caribe

Específicos:

I. Desarrollar mecanismos y metodologías para hacer más expedito y asequible el flujo documental sobre planificación generado en la región

II. Coordinar y desarrollar actividades de apoyo técnico y capacitación requeridos por los centros participantes

III. Mantener en la sede de CEPAL/CLADES una base de datos bibliográficos regional y actualizada sobre planificación

Con la finalidad de dimensionar el proyecto de manera realista, se convocó en 1979 a dos reuniones de expertos en planificación y en ciencias de la información, en las que se discutieron y definieron los siguientes aspectos:[25]

I. Definición del sistema según las necesidades de los usuarios. Se integró el universo de usuarios mediante el conjunto de autoridades, profesionales, investigadores y técnicos participantes en las diversas etapas del proceso de planificación.

II. Limites del sistema:

a. Documentación—tipo y volumen de la información a ingresar

b. Alcance geográfico—nacional-regional-mundial

c. Idiomas abarcados—para la documentación se definió, en una primera etapa, el ingreso de documentos en español, inglés, francés y portugués. Para el caso del sistema, se definieron para una primera fase, español e inglés.

III. Aspectos técnicos. Utilizar la capacidad tecnológica instalada y recursos humanos especializados existentes en cada uno de los componentes del sistema.

    a. Almacenamiento físico de la información. Se definió formar una colección básica centralizada en la sede de CLADES, en Santiago, Chile y en el Centro de Documentación del Caribe (CDC) en Puerto España.

    b. Criterios para el tratamiento de la información. Se adoptó la utilización del sistema ISIS (*Integrated Set of Information Systems*) para el control y recuperación de la información en la base de datos bibliográficos sobre planificación.

IV. Apoyo técnico al sistema. Integrado por actividades de capacitación, asesoramiento técnico, herramientas técnicas y definición del tipo de resúmenes.

    a. Actividades de capacitación. Destinada al personal de los diversos organismos regionales involucrados.

        i. A corto plazo: CLADES e ILPES prepararon cursos básicos de información y documentación en Santiago, Chile

        ii. A largo plazo: Realizar cursos de actualización en información y documentación en algunos países del sistema, de acuerdo a sus solicitudes

    b. Asesoramiento técnico.

        i. Establecer programas de asesoramiento de acuerdo con las características y nivel de la infraestructura de los centros cooperadores y ofrecer el asesoramiento según la etapa del programa en ejecución

        ii. Promover la cooperación técnica horizontal con el objeto de descentralizar gradualmente las actividades

    c. Elaboración de herramientas técnicas.

        i. Vocabularios controlados. Para una primera etapa se acordó utilizar el Macrothesaurus de la OCDE, el cual se enriquecería con terminología propia de planificación para satisfacer las necesidades de información específica y propia de América Latina y el Caribe.

d. Definición del tipo de resúmenes.

i. Con el propósito de ofrecer una herramienta de ayuda para que el usuario seleccionara las fuentes de información de su interés, se decidió ingresar a la base de datos resúmenes de tipo indicativo e informativo, redactados de manera libre y con los descriptores fuera del texto.

Productos y servicios del proyecto[26]

Para la difusión de la información contenida en la base de datos se publicó *PLANINDEX, Boletín de Resúmenes Semestral* elaborado por CEPAL/ CLADES. En dicho boletín, el usuario podía acceder a la información por materias, autores personales e institucionales, por países y por categorías donde se representaban las diversas etapas del proceso de planificación.

Para su distribución se elaboró un estudio sobre las principales instituciones relacionadas con el proceso de planificación. Hacia 1982 se distribuían poco más de cuatrocientos ejemplares en instituciones de América Latina, el Caribe, Europa, África y Asia.

Para la difusión de las actividades del INFOPLAN y una selección de publicaciones recientes se utilizó también el Boletín de planificación del ILPES, a partir de 1982.

Los servicios directos a usuarios consistieron en:

I. Elaboración de bibliografías especializadas

II. Búsquedas retrospectivas de información en la base de datos

III. Reproducción de documentos

Las publicaciones derivadas del proyecto fueron:

I. INFOPLAN: Manual de selección de documentos

II. INFOPLAN: Manual de capacitación. Curso básico

III. Curso de administración de redes y unidades de información

IV. Guía para el uso del Macrothesaurus

V. INFOPLAN. Categorías DEVSIS. Esquema clasificatorio y conceptual

Herramientas para el trabajo documental

El trabajo de especialistas en información tuvo como uno de sus resultados la preparación de varias herramientas para el trabajo documental, entre las que se cuentan:

I. Manuales para el manejo de bases de datos y programas de computación bibliográficos

II. Manuales para el ingreso de datos y de indización, hojas de registro y de análisis de información, fichas de registro de descriptores y su manual de uso

III. Cuestionarios y formularios para encuestas y otras actividades de investigación

Mención especial merece la participación del CLADES en la revisión de la versión española del Macrothesaurus de la OCDE. Fue designado también como organismo regional coordinador de las actividades relacionadas con la elaboración de tesauros en América Latina. Para cumplir con tales fines desarrolló, entre otras, las siguientes actividades:

I. Incorporación de la terminología latinoamericana al Macrothesaurus de la OCDE

II. Revisión constante de la terminología en el campo socioeconómico producida en otras regiones para establecer su compatibilización o equivalencia

III. Recepción de lenguajes sectoriales producidos en la región para su revisión, control y compatibilización con el Macrothesaurus[27]

Las publicaciones del CLADES

Los resultados del trabajo del CLADES a lo largo de más de treinta años se han vertido en un conjunto de más de doscientos publicaciones. En términos generales, pueden clasificarse temáticamente en los siguientes once rubros:

I. Asistencia técnica

II. Bibliografías especializadas

III. Capacitación

IV. Cooperación y políticas de información

V. Desarrollo de unidades y redes de información

VI. Directorios

VII. Documentos informativos—CLADES

VIII. Documentos informativos—Proyectos

IX. Documentos informativos—Reuniones

X. Gestión de la información

XI. Terminología y tesauros[28]

Por lo que respecta a las publicaciones periódicas, se cuenta con *Cladindex: resúmenes de documentos CEPAL/ILPES,* la primera publicación con resúmenes de los trabajos generados por la CEPAL, publicado entre 1977 y 1979. A partir de 1980 y hasta 1997, se denominó *Cepalindex: resúmenes de trabajos del sistema CEPAL,* que incluye un volumen acumulativo comprendido entre los años 1948 a 1997.

Para registrar la producción documental en planificación, se publicaron entre 1980 y 1996, dieciséis volúmenes de *Planindex: resúmenes de documentos sobre planificación.*

Es posible obtener información referencial de los documentos a través del catálogo de la Biblioteca de la CEPAL.[29] Para el caso de algunos documentos, es ofrecido el acceso al texto completo.

Actividades de cara al nuevo milenio

A partir del inicio de los años noventa, el CLADES se dio a la tarea de estudiar otros aspectos en el campo de la información, entre ellos, la interacción sistema-usuario, el alcance de las nuevas formas de información y en particular, los productos de información con valor agregado. Por otra parte, y con base en un proceso de autoanálisis, se determinó enfocar las actividades del Centro a "la investigación, estudio y discusión de documentación relevante en materias como: teoría administrativa y política de las organizaciones, ambiente organizacional de los sistemas formales e informales de información, perfil del nuevo profesional, recursos tecnológicos y telecomunicaciones."[30]

Uno de los productos del CLADES en los últimos años ha sido la definición de un curso de gestión de información, orientado al estudio de los temas concernientes al contexto de las organizaciones y al ámbito de las infraestructuras de información, con la finalidad de cambiar la óptica para el análisis de los fenómenos informacionales.[31]

Conclusiones

No cabe duda que los esfuerzos para desarrollar el sistema de información para la planeación constituyeron un factor importante para el desarrollo de la región. Se trató de un sistema sólido que contemplaba los distintos aspectos del manejo de la información. Si analizamos los productos derivados del proyecto, podemos advertir que los servicios y publicaciones respondieron siempre a necesidades claramente planteadas por académicos de las áreas de la economía y la sociología, y que la intervención de especialistas en el manejo de la información le dio solidez al diseño e integración de bases de datos para el manejo de la información, lo cual permitió, posteriormente, la creación de herramientas impresas para acceder a la información producida en las distintas áreas de la CEPAL.

Cuando se analiza la documentación existente sobre el diseño del proyecto para constituir el sistema de información para el desarrollo, se advierte la existencia de un proceso de planeación sistemática, con productos claramente definidos en cada una de las partes del proceso.[32] El estudio de dicha documentación permite reconstruir y visualizar el desarrollo de los sistemas de información durante el último tercio del siglo veinte.

Varios de los productos del CLADES constituyeron la base para la posterior automatización de las bibliotecas de la región. El sistema MicroIsis por ejemplo, y herramientas como CEPALINDEX o PLANINDEX, aún hoy en día son fuentes de información valiosa para la investigación económica y social de América Latina y el Caribe.

NOTAS

1. Centro Latinoamericano de Documentación Económica y Social, *CLADES: su rol y funciones*, 1.

2. Santa Cruz, *La CEPAL*, 11–12.

3. Ibid., 17.

4. Ibid., 27.

5. Comisión Económica para América Latina y el Caribe, "Información General."

6. Centro Latinoamericano de Documentación Económica y Social, *Un sistema de información*, 3.

7. Ibid., 33.

8. Riquelme, *CLADES: 25 años de investigación y acción*, 11–12.

9. Centro Latinoamericano, *CLADES: su rol y funciones*, 1.

10. Riquelme, *CLADES: 25 años de investigación y acción*, 12–13.

11. Ibid., 17.

12. Centro Latinoamericano, *CLADES: su rol y funciones*, 3.

13. Adaptado de Centro Latinoamericano, *CLADES: su rol y funciones*, Anexo 1.

14. Riquelme, *CLADES: 25 años de investigación y acción*, 18.

15. Ibid., 20–21.

16. Ibid., 21.

17. Ibid., 22.

18. Ibid., 23.

19. Comisión Económica para América Latina y el Caribe, *CLADES*, 12–13.

20. Ibid., 2–3.

21. Centro Latinoamericano, *CLADES: su rol y funciones*, 1.

22. Comisión Económica, *CLADES*, 4.

23. Centro Latinoamericano, *Un sistema de información*, 2.

24. Centro Latinoamericano, *El sistema INFOPLAN*, 2.

25. Centro Latinoamericano, *Un sistema de información*, 15–23.

26. Centro Latinoamericano, *El sistema INFOPLAN*, 16–17.

27. Riquelme, *CLADES: 25 años de investigación y acción*, 32–33.

28. Ibid., 49–76. Una selección de los documentos correspondientes a cada uno de los rubros aparece como anexo.

29. http://www.biblioteca.cepal.org/.

30. Riquelme, *CLADES: 25 años de investigación y acción*, 41.

31. Ibid.

32. Centro Latinoamericano, *Un sistema de información*, 57–87.

BIBLIOGRAFÍA

Centro Latinoamericano de Documentación Económica y Social. *CLADES: su rol y funciones.* Santiago, Chile: Comisión Económica para América Latina, 1977.

————. Un sistema de información *para la planificación en América Latina y el Caribe: instrumento fundamental para la coordinación y cooperación entre países en desarrollo.* Santiago, Chile: Comisión Económica para América Latina, 1979.

————. *El sistema INFOPLAN: estructura, funciones y operación.* Santiago, Chile: Comisión Económica para América Latina, 1982.

Comisión Económica para América Latina. *CLADES: una contribución para América Latina y El Caribe en el campo de la información para el desarrollo.* Santiago, Chile: Comisión Económica para América Latina, 1982.

————. "Información general." Modificada por última vez el 7 de abril 2012. http://www.eclac.org/cgi-bin/getprod.asp?xml=/noticias/paginas/4/21324/P21324. xml&xsl=/tpl/p18f-st.xsl&base=/tpl/top-bottom_acerca.xsl.

Riquelme, Rigoberta. *CLADES: 25 años de investigación y acción.* Santiago, Chile: Comisión Económica para América Latina, 1996.

Santa Cruz, Hernán. *La CEPAL: encarnación de una esperanza de América Latina.* Santiago, Chile: Comisión Económica para América Latina, 1985.

13. Políticas de adquisición bibliográfica en la República de Chile

Sergio Rodríguez Quezada

Introducción

Chile es un pequeño país sudamericano con diecisiete millones de habitantes aproximadamente, 4,270 kilómetros de longitud, y una concentración urbana superior al 83 por ciento.[1] Cuenta con una población orgullosa de los procesos democráticos alcanzados en los últimos veinte años y con altos índices de probidad administrativa, señalados en numerosos estudios sobre el tema. Como ejemplo se puede señalar que Chile ocupa el lugar veintitrés entre 180 países según el Índice de Percepción de Corrupción del año 2008 que elabora Transparencia Internacional, y el primer lugar en América Latina junto a Uruguay.[2]

Su ingreso per cápita para el año 2010, de acuerdo al Fondo Monetario Internacional (FMI), es de US$14,299, con un crecimiento de 560 por ciento en los últimos treinta años, y siendo el más alto de América Latina.[3] En contraparte, la distribución de la riqueza es dramáticamente desigual, obteniendo el 10 por ciento más rico de la población el 40 por ciento de los ingresos y el 10 por ciento más pobre solo el 1 por ciento de esos ingresos.[4] Los últimos estudios sobre situación socioeconómica nos indican que un 15.1 por ciento de la población se encuentra en situación de pobreza (25.6 por ciento en 1990) y un 3.7 por ciento en indigencia (13 por ciento en 1990).[5]

Esta realidad y la preocupación por superarla han generado, por parte del estado, numerosas políticas de integración social, entre las que destacaremos las del ámbito del fomento a la lectura. La cual por su parte ha permitido realizar una profunda trasformación en los procedimientos administrativos, incorporando la tecnología y capital humano requerido para estos cambios. Serán estos nuevos procedimientos los que abordaremos a continuación, en particular la descripción del servicio ChileCompra Libros y su impacto en la disponibilidad de material bibliográfico para su adquisición.

ChileCompra

La organización conocida como ChileCompra (http://www.chilecompra. cl) inició su funcionamiento el año 2001, como parte de los proyectos de Gobierno Digital impulsados por la administración central de la época, bajo

la presidencia de Ricardo Lagos Escobar, cuyo principal objetivo era moder-
nizar y transparentar las compras públicas, centralizando su accionar y eco-
nomizando en sus procedimientos. La experiencia fue tomada de países como
España, Noruega y Francia, entre otros.

En este contexto, se entiende por compra pública todos los contratos que
suscribe el gobierno para la adquisición de bienes, servicios y obras públicas,
desde los más complejos, como la construcción de carreteras, hasta los de
baja complejidad, como la compra de lápices o en el caso que atrae nuestra
atención, material bibliográfico para políticas públicas de fomento a la lectura, bibliotecas públicas, fuerzas armadas, gobiernos locales y universidades
dependientes del estado, entre otras organizaciones.

El sistema ChileCompra señala: "Nuestra misión es crear valor en el
Mercado Público, para que los compradores del Estado puedan hacer su trabajo cada día de manera más transparente y eficiente y que los proveedores
tengan más facilidad de acceso. Nuestro trabajo está enfocado en nuestros
clientes, asegurando un alta calidad, y usando de manera intensiva las tecnologías de información."[6]

Este sistema ha tenido un sostenido crecimiento a lo largo de los años,
llegando a generar sistemas especializados para atender las demandas cada
vez más específicas de las instituciones que componen el estado. Entre otros
servicios se destacan: Compras Sustentables, ChileCompra Express, Yo Elijo
mi PC, y ChileCompra Libros, siendo éste último el que analizaremos con más
detalle.

ChileCompra Libros

La mayor parte de las adquisiciones de material bibliográfico por parte
de instituciones estatales se realiza a través del sistema ChileCompra Libros
(http://www.chilecompralibros.cl), el cual nació el año 2008 como respuesta
a la necesidad de suministrar un servicio especializado para la gestión de la
adquisición de colecciones en soporte impreso y digital, generando mayores
facilidades tanto para las instituciones del estado como para sus proveedores.

En la definición de sus servicios señala: "Somos una Tienda virtual en
Internet a través de la cual todos los organismos públicos—instituciones del
gobierno central, municipalidades, hospitales, fuerzas armadas y de orden y
universidades, pueden visualizar una gran gama de títulos y adquirir con un
solo clic libros, CDs, DVDs y publicaciones."[7]

De acuerdo a lo señalado en la ley N° 19.886 sobre compras públicas
se incorporan obligatoriamente al sistema desde ese año el Ministerio de
Educación (MINEDUC) y la Dirección de Bibliotecas Archivos y Museos
(DIBAM), los mayores compradores de material y los cuales representaron
en el año 2009 más del 90 por ciento de las adquisiciones por este concepto a
nivel estatal.

En este sistema participaron 339 compradores hasta fines de 2009, principalmente gobiernos locales y setenta y ocho proveedores que se mantienen inalterados dado el complejo sistema de inscripción.

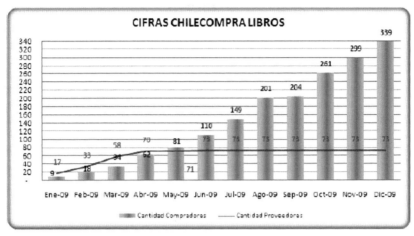

Figura 1. Cifras ChileCompra Libros: compradores, proveedores
Fuente: ChileCompra Libros, "Mesa de Trabajo con Asociaciones Gremiales de Libros"

En el año 2009, se adquirieron US$46,876,000 en material bibliográfico, principalmente libros impresos, para apoyo del proceso educativo, literatura general en el caso del proyecto Maletín Literario, y para bibliotecas de colegios y liceos, programas que describiremos desde el punto de vista de la adquisición del material.

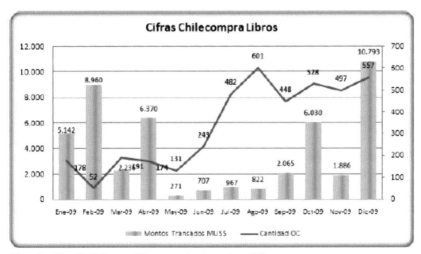

Figura 2. Cifras ChileCompra Libros: montos transados y OC
Fuente: ChileCompra Libros, "Mesa de Trabajo con Asociaciones Gremiales de Libros"

Funcionamiento ChileCompra Libros

Este catálogo electrónico incorpora proveedores de libros, música, películas, documentales, periódicos, diarios y revistas que ofrecen precios con descuentos y cobertura de distribución nacional de sus productos. Para tener la condición de proveedor, se requiere que previamente haya sido adjudicada una licitación pública, efectuada por la Dirección de ChileCompra a través del sistema http://www.MercadoPublico.cl.

Esta experiencia es inédita en relación a la venta de bienes culturales en nuestro país y busca transformarse en un espacio de encuentro virtual para la cultura nacional y universal, beneficiando a la comunidad y al sistema de educación pública chilena en todos sus niveles, al facilitar la compra de estos productos por parte del estado, permitiendo una mayor eficiencia y planificación de las compras de material bibliográfico.

Se proyecta que esta tienda virtual cuente a finales del 2010 con más de sesenta mil títulos disponibles. Actualmente ya se encuentran catalogados al mes de mayo 40,823 títulos en las cinco categorías indicadas: libros, música, películas, periódicos y revistas.

Los setenta y ocho proveedores disponibles, se desglosan en: cincuenta y cinco de libros, veinticinco de revistas y diarios, doce de películas y ocho de música, siendo permitido que un proveedor participe en varias de estas categorías simultáneamente. Se debe tomar en cuenta que esta cifra incluye materiales editados en cualquier formato, soporte, nacionalidad del autor y contenido y no solo libros de autores nacionales.

Los productos que ofrece ChileCompra Libros son los siguientes:

- Libros impresos o por medios electrónicos. Algunas de las temáticas son literatura (novela, poesía, teatro, cuento, ensayo, etc.), ciencias y tecnología (medicina, genética, computación, etc.), ciencias sociales (economía, administración, psicología, política, derecho, etc.), diccionarios, enciclopedias, arte, música, fotografía, humor, cómic, pasatiempo, infantiles y didácticos, textos de estudio, libros en braille, material didáctico, etc., siendo este esquema fruto de la creatividad de algún funcionario y no del desarrollo de un esquema que represente todas las áreas del conocimiento.

- Música en soporte físico o digital. Las temáticas abordan música clásica, música de películas y TV, jazz, blues y *black music,* rock y pop, entre otros.

- Películas o documentales. Incluye películas y documentales chilenos, drama y comedia, musicales y conciertos, infantiles y dibujos animados, deporte, educación, etc.

- Diarios y revistas impresos o digitales, ya sean nacionales o extranjeros. Se incorporan diarios regionales y nacionales, educación, literatura, música, idiomas, finanzas, negocios y economía, salud y medicina y nutrición, entre otros.

Entre los beneficios que ChileCompra Libros pretende entregar como institución se pueden destacar que:

- Los compradores públicos obtienen un canal más expedito, eficiente y transparente disponible permanentemente para adquirir artículos dentro de cada rubro.

- Se ahorra dinero fiscal al eliminar el trámite administrativo para cada licitación.

- Se permite la descentralización de la elección de la compra y la centralización en el pago. Los bibliotecarios, encargados de bibliotecas o desarrolladores de colecciones, académicos y otros interesados, podrán elegir sus títulos directamente desde la tienda y traspasar su necesidad al responsable de adquisiciones.

- Los compradores tienen acceso a ofertas especiales.

- Se pueden agregar títulos que no estén disponibles en la base de datos exhortando a todos los proveedores para que los incorporen (únicamente entre los setenta y ocho proveedores disponibles).

- Se permiten compras a través de la modalidad del procedimiento "Compras Mayores," superiores a US$55,000 como una forma de mejorar el precio de compra.

- Los proveedores de medios escritos y audiovisuales, que fueron adjudicados a través de la modalidad de convenio marco, suministran los libros, DVDs y CDs en condiciones ventajosas y a precios competitivos.

- Todos los estudiantes de escuelas y colegios públicos de Chile dispondrán en plazos más reducidos y con garantías de calidad del material escrito y audiovisual para apoyar y complementar su proceso educativo.

- Los profesores de colegios y universidades estatales podrán recurrir al catálogo para adquirir los materiales necesarios para sus actividades.

- Los administradores y gestores del sistema público de educación ven maximizados los recursos de los que disponen y obtienen productos culturales con las mejores condiciones de precio, calidad y despacho.

- Por último, la ciudadanía en general también se beneficia al obtener ahorros de los recursos fiscales comprometidos.

Para adquirir el material bibliográfico a través de este convenio, están disponibles tres mecanismos diferentes de compras al que pueden acceder los compradores:

1. Compra directa de títulos disponibles en la tienda virtual

2. Cotización para títulos que no se encuentran en la tienda y su inclusión en la misma

3. Procedimiento de licitación para compras mayores a US$55,000

Para adquirir los productos bibliográficos se debe contar con una clave que es entregada por la organización ChileCompra a cada organismo público y que permite generar órdenes de compra en línea a cada proveedor y administrar los montos de compra. Cualquier usuario del sitio puede ingresar en la opción visitante, navegar a través de la tienda y conocer su oferta de productos. No podrá, sin embargo, realizar compras de los mismos a través del sistema, pero sí obtener los datos del distribuidor en Chile.

Principales programas de adquisición de material bibliográfico del Gobierno de Chile en el año 2009

Los programas que se reseñan a continuación dan cuenta de la relevancia del sistema ChileCompra Libros en la licitación y adjudicación de grandes volúmenes de libros para la ejecución de las políticas de gobierno.

Maletín Literario

El Programa Maletín Literario, anunciado por la Presidente Michelle Bachelet durante el Mensaje Presidencial del 21 de mayo del 2007, tenía por objetivo contribuir a fomentar la lectura en las familias que viven en condiciones de pobreza mediante la entrega de una biblioteca familiar que permitiera un primer acercamiento al libro. Se aplicó los años 2008 y 2009, sin continuidad en el 2010 por reasignación presupuestaria de los fondos a la reconstrucción, luego del terremoto del 27 de febrero de 2010 que afectó al centro sur del país.

Este proyecto trató, al inicio, de proveer de una Biblioteca Básica Familiar con acciones de fomento a la lectura desde la escuela y la biblioteca pública, esperando incrementar significativamente el hábito de la lectura en todos los integrantes del grupo familiar. En este proyecto se invirtieron US$14.5 millones entre los años 2008 y 2009, constituyendo el mayor programa de adquisición de libros hasta la fecha, con un total de 5,684,000 ejemplares distribuidos en grupos de catorce o quince unidades por beneficiario, llegando a 425,000 familias en riesgo social.[8]

Gracias al volumen de la compra, el valor promedio de cada libro fue de US$2.55, muy por debajo de los precios al público de las obras seleccionadas. Entre las obras adquiridas se incluye un diccionario enciclopédico y un atlas.

Centro de Recursos del Aprendizaje (CRA)

En el año 1994, frente a la necesidad de crear un mejor entorno para los estudiantes, se concretó la realización del proyecto Bibliotecas CRA. Por medio del cual se pretendía redimensionar el rol que hasta ese momento habían tenido las bibliotecas en nuestro país a través de la implementación de bibliotecas escolares para la educación media. Este programa fue una estrategia del programa Mejoramiento de la Calidad de la Educación (MECE Media).

El programa MECE Media consideró crear o actualizar una biblioteca en cada uno de los planteles educativos con financiamiento del estado, y promover su transformación progresiva, desde su estructura escolar más sencilla, hasta bibliotecas más complejas que llegaran a conformar Centros de Recursos para el Aprendizaje (CRA) con el potencial de prestar servicios educativos y culturales más allá de la comunidad escolar en que se insertaran. La colección de libros y otros recursos comprendía más de mil títulos por establecimiento y se adquirió y distribuyó en tres etapas, la última de las cuales fue durante el año 2002.

A partir del año 2003 y estando cubierta casi toda la enseñanza media, el componente Bibliotecas Escolares CRA ha dirigido su accionar a cumplir el compromiso ministerial de llegar al bicentenario con cobertura cercana al 100 por ciento de bibliotecas CRA en la enseñanza básica municipalizada y particular subvencionada. Como resultado de estas políticas, al año 2010 existen 6,336 bibliotecas escolares básicas y 1,919 de enseñanza media, faltando aproximadamente 1,000 establecimientos por implementar con bibliotecas.

Durante los años 2008 y 2009 el presupuesto anual del programa fue de US$11,327,000, destinando más del 65 por ciento de esos recursos a la compra de material bibliográfico. Destaca en este sentido la licitación de más de un millón de libros realizada hasta fines del 2009 por un monto total de US$7.5 millones, beneficiando a las bibliotecas escolares de todo el país. El valor final por libro no superó los US$7.50, aún tratándose de libros álbum, de formato color y tapas duras, lo cual encarece su costo, pero también los hace más atractivos a los estudiantes. Este programa es el de más larga aplicación como política de estado, para el desarrollo de sistemas de bibliotecas, capacitación de personal y la adquisición de material bibliográfico.[9]

Ministerio de Educación (MINEDUC)

El mayor comprador por parte del estado es el MINEDUC, que por medio de su Programa de Textos Escolares en todos los niveles de educación, licita textos de estudio para el apoyo de los procesos educativos. Estas compras son de carácter anual y representaron durante el año 2008 una inversión de US$24.6 millones, y de US$328 millones durante el 2009 (un incremento del 33 por ciento),[10] duplicándose en los últimos seis años el presupuesto en esta área. El MINEDUC es entonces un importante cliente de grandes editoriales y empresas impresoras multinacionales con presencia en Chile. A modo de ejemplo, se pueden apreciar en el sector noticias del sitio http://www. chilecompralibros.cl las condiciones de licitación de cincuenta y dos mil textos para el área de física en la enseñanza media. El valor promedio de un libro de texto adjudicado mediante este sistema de licitación es de US$36, según lo informado por el MINEDUC.

Evaluación proceso de instalación ChileCompra Libros

Como parte del proceso de reflexión sobre el funcionamiento del sistema, realizaremos una evaluación de su primer año de funcionamiento, analizando los principales componentes del mismo y su impacto en el sistema de comercialización del material bibliográfico.

Fortalezas

- Generación de una herramienta de búsqueda o catálogo que permita tanto a las editoriales como a los distribuidores locales difundir el material bibliográfico disponible en Chile, apoyando su comercialización tanto en el país como en el extranjero.

- Mayores posibilidades de selección de material para pequeños compradores alejados de los centros urbanos y con reducidas opciones de acceso a las grandes cadenas editoriales.

- Automatización de los procesos administrativos relacionados con la adquisición de material bibliográfico en organismos públicos, facilitando su gestión.

- Menores tiempos de obtención del material bibliográfico gracias al rápido proceso de selección, adjudicación e información al proveedor de la compra realizada.

Oportunidades

- El crecimiento en la participación de organismos del estado como compradores, mediante la difusión del servicio y sus beneficios. En la actualidad son 339 los organismos del estado participantes en el sitio como compradores, teniendo la posibilidad de crecer más de un 100 por ciento en los próximos años.

- Crecimiento de nuevos oferentes, lo cual se puede lograr flexibilizando los procedimientos de inscripción al sistema, tanto en los requisitos que se deben cumplir como los plazos para este fin.

Debilidades

- La existencia de no más de cuarenta y un mil títulos ingresados en el sistema genera una dificultad al momento de seleccionar material, afectando esta baja oferta la diversidad de contenidos para adquirir, dirigiendo la compra hacia aquellos títulos existentes en la base, lo que puede generar problemas de desarrollo de las colecciones que requieren una mayor *bibliodiversidad* lingüística, idiomática, cultural o editorial.

- La lenta actualización de los catálogos editoriales en el sistema ChileCompra Libros, en promedio tres meses, según lo indicado por diversas fuentes editoriales, como consecuencia de la centralización del proceso de ingreso de datos bibliográficos, el cual solo lo realiza la administración del sistema, lo que impide un rápido acceso a las novedades editoriales.

- El escaso control de existencia de inventario que muestra el sistema, genera que los requerimientos realizados a los proveedores no siempre encuentren la respuesta de acuerdo a la información existente, generando la anulación de órdenes de compra y la sustitución de títulos por otros menos requeridos por las bibliotecas.

- En el ingreso de información al catálogo se utilizan, para su estructura de materias, categorías que no tienen relación con la organización del conocimiento utilizada clásicamente en bibliotecología, generando al momento de la recuperación y visualización de la información bibliográfica por materia, errores de relevancia que afectan la credibilidad de la herramienta.

- La no consideración de la adquisición de material bibliográfico de valor histórico o patrimonial en el sistema, lo que imposibilita su gestión.

- Debilitamiento de la cadena de distribución. La creación del sistema, afectó a pequeños distribuidores de sectores alejados del centro administrativo, concentrando la venta y distribución en los centros urbanos, principalmente la capital, Santiago, de donde son el 95 por ciento de los proveedores, ayudando a la centralización económica y afectando la competitividad de quienes están fuera del sistema y como efecto de esto, generando una disminución de los actores en la cadena de distribución de libros al mercado particular. Esta situación es especialmente preocupante dados los datos entregados por la Cámara Chilena del Libro, los cuales informan que solo treinta y cuatro librerías asociadas a esta organización están presentes en las regiones del país.[11]

- El sistema de selección de títulos tiende a premiar a los autores más vendidos, con una mayor cobertura en los medios y presencia en el imaginario colectivo, disminuyendo la ya difícil comercialización de las autoediciones y autores emergentes o sin convenio de distribución con alguno de los proveedores actuales de ChileCompra Libros.

Amenazas

- La lentitud en la actualización puede generar la migración de compradores a otros sistemas o formas de adquisición que les aseguren la obtención de las novedades editoriales en menor tiempo.

- Concentración de la adquisición en pocos proveedores, setenta y ocho en total, como consecuencia de los requisitos y procedimientos para la aceptación como tal, ya que para ser proveedor se debe postular a una licitación pública donde se exige cumplir con requisitos que difícilmente puede satisfacer un pequeño distribuidor, relacionadas con montos de facturación y capacidad logística entre otras. Se espera que en el año 2010 se genere un nuevo proceso de selección que permita aumentar el número de proveedores participantes.

Recomendaciones

- Reevaluar el sistema de adquisición de material bibliográfico cuando se trate de montos menores a los US$5,000 por título, permitiendo una gestión de compra directa con los proveedores presentes en el mercado nacional e internacional. Esto evitaría la concentración de las adquisiciones en pocos proveedores y permitiría un mejor desarrollo de los fondos bibliográficos.

- Mantener el sistema para grandes licitaciones de libros de texto escolar vinculados al apoyo educacional y para la compra de títulos en miles de copias, usados frecuentemente en la distribución de material de lectura entre la población como parte de programas de fomento a la lectura. En ambos casos se ha demostrado que los precios de compra final resultaron ser beneficiosos para el estado.

- Ampliar el número de proveedores mediante la apertura total del sistema o la modificación de las bases de postulación y aceptación, dando mayores facilidades para la participación de otros actores del mercado.

- Incorporar a bibliotecólogos, libreros y editores en el necesario proceso de restructuración de su base de datos bibliográfica, incorporando métodos bibliotecológicos en la estructuración de la información, tanto en el ingreso como en la recuperación y visualización de los datos.

- Permitir la incorporación directa de la información por parte de las editoriales y su publicación previa validación del contenido en el sistema por ChileCompra Libros.

NOTAS

1. Gobierno de Chile, *Encuesta de caracterización socioeconómica nacional.*
2. Gobierno de Chile, "Preguntas frecuentes."

3. Bermejo, "Chile liderará PIB."
4. Toro, "La distribución de ingresos en Chile."
5. Gobierno de Chile, *Encuesta de caracterización socioeconómica nacional.*
6. Gobierno de Chile, "Definiciones estratégicas."
7. Ministerio de Hacienda. Definición visto el 15 de julio 2010,
http://www.chilecompralibros.cl/ChileCompraLibros/tabid/57/language/es-CL/Default.aspx.
8. Gobierno de Chile. *Memoria,* 71–80.
9. Gobierno de Chile, *Propuesta estándares,* 41. Consultar también http://www.
bibliotecas-cra.cl/quienes/quie_hist.html.
10. Libertad y Desarrollo, "Minuta presupuesto de educación."
11. Cámara Chilena del Libro, "Guía de librerías."

BIBLIOGRAFÍA

Bermeo, Miguel. "Chile liderará PIB." *Diario La Tercera*, 10 de febrero 2009. http://latercera.com/contenido/745_188564_9.shtml.

Cámara Chilena del Libro. "Guía de librerías." Modificada por última vez el 27 de febrero 2012. http://www.camaradellibro.cl/guia_librerias.htm.

ChileCompra Libros. "Mesa de Trabajo con Asociaciones Gremiales de Libros: Reunión Periódica 07/2009; 28 diciembre 2009."Accedido el 16 de julio 2010. http://www.chilecompralibros.cl/LinkClick.aspx?fileticket=tNb%2FQPIyXJw%3D&tabid=56&language=....

Gobierno de Chile. "Definiciones estratégicas de la dirección ChileCompra años 2012–2014." Ministerio de Hacienda. Modificada por última vez el 25 de abril 2012. http://www.chilecompra.cl/index.php?option=com_content&view=article&id=69&Itemid=175.

Gobierno de Chile. *Memoria dirección de bibliotecas archivos y museos: 2008/2009.* DIBAM: Santiago, 2009.

Gobierno de Chile, Ministerio de Educación. *Propuesta estándares para las bibliotecas escolares CRA.* MINEDUC: Santiago, 2010.

Gobierno de Chile, Ministerio de Planificación y Cooperación. *Encuesta de caracterización socioeconómica nacional.* Santiago, 2009. http://www.mideplan.cl/casen2009/.

Gobierno de Chile. "Preguntas frecuentes." Consejo de Alta Dirección. Modificada por última vez el 25 de abril 2012. http://www.serviciocivil.gob.cl/programa-chile-probidad/preguntas-frecuentes-5.

Libertad y Desarrollo. "Minuta Presupuesto de Educación 2009."Visto el 16 de julio 2010. http://www.lyd.com/lyd/controls/neochannels/neo_ch4311/deploy/minuta_educacion_2009%20v2.pdf.

Toro, Rodrigo. "La distribución de ingresos en Chile." Modificada por última vez el 7 de abril 2012. http://www.monografias.com/trabajos17/distribucion-ingreso-chile/distribucion-ingreso-chile.shtml.

Contributors

Claire-Lise Bénaud, University of New Mexico

Micaela Chávez Villa, Colegio de México

Víctor J. Cid Carmona, Colegio de México

Georgette M. Dorn, U.S. Library of Congress

Mark L. Grover, Brigham Young University

Kathleen Helenese-Paul, University of the West Indies, St. Augustine

Deborah Jakubs, Duke University

Ellen Jaramillo, Yale University

Molly Molloy, New Mexico State University

David C. Murray, Temple University

Álvaro Risso, Librería Linardi y Risso

Sergio Rodríguez Quezada, Universidad Bolivariana and Dirección de Bibliotecas, Archivos y Museos, Chile

Luis Rodríguez Yunta, Consejo Superior de Investigaciones Científicas (CSIC) and Centro de Ciencias Humanas y Sociales (CCHS), Spain

C. Denise Stuempfle, Indiana University

Conference Program

Friday, July 23, 2010

8:00 A.M.–5:00 P.M.	Registration
9:00–10:00 A.M.	New Members Orientation
9:00–10:00 A.M.	Committee Meetings Nominations Cuban Bibliography
9:00–11:00 A.M.	Finance Committee Meeting #1
10:00–11:00 A.M.	Bibliographic Instruction ENLACE/Outreach
11:00 A.M.–noon	Electronic Resources Membership
Noon–1:30 P.M.	Lunch
1:30–3:00 P.M.	Regional Group Meetings CALAFIA (California Cooperative Latin American Collection Development Group) LANE (Latin America North East Libraries Consortium) LASER (Latin American Studies Southeast Region) MOLLAS (Midwest Organization of Libraries for Latin American Studies)
3:00–4:00 P.M.	Cuba Working Group Initiative
3:00–4:00 P.M.	Committee Meetings Audio-Visual Serials
4:00–5:00 P.M.	Editorial Board Interlibrary Cooperation ALZAR (Academic Latino/a Zone of Action and Research)
5:00–6:00 P.M.	Committee Meetings Reference Services Policy, Research and Investigation Medina Award
6:00–7:00 P.M.	New Members and ENLACE Happy Hour
7:00–9:30 P.M.	LAMP

Saturday, July 24, 2010

8:00 A.M.–5:00 P.M.	Registration
9:00–11:00 A.M.	Latin American Research Resources Project (LARRP)
9:00–10:00 A.M.	Committee Meetings Cataloging and Bibliographic Technology
10:00–11:00 A.M.	Gifts and Exchanges Libreros Committee Meeting
11:00 A.M.–noon	HAPI Marginalized Peoples and Ideas Official Publications
Noon–1:30 P.M.	Lunch
1:30–2:30 P.M.	e-SALALM Discussion
1:30–2:30 P.M.	Committee Meetings Constitution and Bylaws
2:30–3:30 P.M.	Access and Bibliography Acquisitions Library Operations and Services
1:30–4:00 P.M.	Bookdealer/Librarian Consultations
4:00–6:00 P.M.	Executive Board Meeting #1
6:30–8:30 P.M.	John Carter Brown Library Reception

Sunday, July 25, 2010

8:00 A.M.–5:00 P.M.	Registration
11:15 A.M.–6:30 P.M.	Book Exhibits
9:00–10:30 A.M.	**Opening Session**
	Rapporteur: *David Block,* University of Texas, Austin
	Welcoming Remarks
	Fernando Acosta-Rodríguez, SALALM President 2009–2010, Princeton University Library
	Patricia Figueroa, SALALM Local Arrangements Chair 2009–2010, Curator of Iberian and Latin American Collections, Brown University Library
	Richard Snyder, Director, Center for Latin American and Caribbean Studies, Brown University
	Harriette Hemmasi, Joukowsky Family University Librarian, Brown University
	Keynote Address
	Deborah Jakubs, Rita DiGiallonardo Holloway University Librarian, Duke University "A Library by Any Other Name: Change, Adaptation, Transformation"
10:30–11:15 A.M.	Book Exhibits Opening Reception

11:15 A.M.–1:00 P.M.	**Panel 1: Envisioning and Shaping the Future of Latin American and Area Studies Collections and Research**
Moderator:	*Nerea Llamas,* University of Michigan, Ann Arbor
Rapporteur:	*Daisy V. Domínguez,* City College of New York, CUNY
Presenters:	*David Block,* University of Texas, Austin "What's Paper Doing in the Electronic Library?"
	Dan Hazen, Harvard University, Cambridge "Area Studies Collections and Research: Boutique Conceits and the Long Tail"
	James Simon, Center for Research Libraries, Chicago "The Future of Collaboration in Area Studies Collections and Research"
1:00–2:00 P.M.	Lunch
2:00–3:45 P.M.	**Panel 2: Traditioned Innovation: Revisiting Partnerships between Libraries and Booksellers**
Moderator:	*Irene Münster,* University of Maryland, Shady Grove
Rapporteur:	*Wendy Louise Pedersen,* University of New Mexico, Albuquerque
Presenters:	*Mark L. Grover,* Brigham Young University, Provo "Don't Try to Change Them: How SALALM's History Provides Insight into the Future of Latin American Studies Library Development"
	Álvaro Risso, Librería Linardi y Risso, Montevideo "¿Qué sabemos del futuro del libro?: el SALALM, los libreros y el libro que está por venir"
	Oscar Puvill, Puvill Libros S.A., Barcelona "Publishers-Bookvendors/Bookvendors-Libraries, Technological Changes on Spanish Titles"
2:00–3:45 P.M.	**Panel 3: Welcome to the Mad Hatter House: Embeddedness and the Evolving Roles of the Latin Americanist Librarians**
Moderator:	*Marisol Ramos,* University of Connecticut, Storrs
Rapporteur:	*Paula Mae Carns,* University of Illinois at Urbana-Champaign
Presenters:	*Marisol Ramos,* University of Connecticut, Storrs "Embedding Latin American Archives into Library Instruction and Practice"
	David C. Murray, Temple University, Philadelphia "Teaching Ancient Mesoamerica: A Collaborative Faculty/Librarian Experiment in Embedment"
	Meiyolet Méndez, University of Miami "The Embedded Librarian from a Collection Development Perspective"
	Melissa Gasparotto, Rutgers University, New Brunswick "Latin American and Iberian Studies Collection Development in the Age of Blogging: Identifying, Collecting and Preserving Literary Blogs"
2:00–3:45 P.M.	**Panel 4: Challenges in Special Collections from the Inquisition to the Digital Age**
Moderator:	*Patricia Figueroa,* Brown University, Providence
Rapporteur:	*Bridget Gazzo,* Dumbarton Oaks Research Library, Washington, D.C.
Presenters:	*Ken Ward,* John Carter Brown Library, Providence "The Private Library of Melchor Pérez de Soto, Mexico, 1650"

Paloma Celis Carbajal, University of Wisconsin, Madison
"It Takes Two to Tango: Opportunities and Challenges with
Collaborative Projects within the Special Collections Environment"

Andrew Ashton, Brown University, Providence
Patricia Figueroa, Brown University, Providence
"Curricular Engagement for Special Collections in the Digital Age"

4:15–6:00 P.M.	**Panel 5: Pecha Kucha: Snapshots of New Trends and Practices**
Moderator:	*Alison Hicks,* University of Colorado, Boulder
Rapporteur:	*Mary Jo Zeter,* Michigan State University, East Lansing
Presenters:	*Katherine D. McCann,* Library of Congress, Washington, D.C. "In Translation: Luring English Speakers to Latin American Studies"

Daisy V. Domínguez, City College of New York, CUNY
"Minga Virtual: How Librarians Can Sow and Harvest on Twitter"

Kent Norsworthy, LANIC, University of Texas, Austin
" 'This Just in…': New and Upcoming Initiatives @UTLANIC"

Martha D. Kelehan, Tufts University, Medford
"GapMinder, GIS, and the Digital Humanities: New Tools for
New Cross-Campus Collaborations"

Orchid Mazurkiewicz, Hispanic American Periodicals Index,
University of California, Los Angeles
"Federated Searching, Data Harvesting, and Latin American Studies"

Daniel M. Schoorl, University of California, Los Angeles
"Data Visualization: Exploring Ideas for Interactivity in SALA Online"

Luis A. González, Indiana University, Bloomington
"Bibliographic Commons: Using Open-Source Citation Management
Software to Create Freely Accessible Online Bibliographic Databases"

4:15–6:00 P.M.	**Panel 6: Quo Vadis? And What Are We Going to Do about It? Roundtable on the Evolving Role of the Latin American Studies Librarian**
Rapporteur:	*Sócrates Silva,* Hispanic American Periodicals Index, University of California, Los Angeles
Coordinators:	*Jesús Alonso-Regalado,* University at Albany, SUNY *Anne Barnhart,* University of West Georgia, Carrolton
4:15–6:00 P.M.	**Panel 7: Implementing New Cataloging Practices and Trends**
Moderator:	*Laura Shedenhelm,* University of Georgia, Athens
Rapporteur:	*Stephanie Rocío Miles,* Harvard University, Cambridge
Presenters:	*John Wright,* Brigham Young University, Provo "A Survey of New Cataloging Trends"

Ana Lupe Cristán, Library of Congress, Washington, D.C.
"RDA: antecedentes y aspectos de su implementación"

Ellen Jaramillo, Yale University, New Haven
"Reading Leonés in New Haven: Cataloging Backlogged Materials in
'Other Iberian Languages' "

7:00–9:00 P.M.	Host Reception, John Hay Library

Monday, July 26, 2010

7:30–9:00 A.M. Finance Committee Meeting #2

8:30 A.M.–4:00 P.M. Registration

8:30 A.M.–6:00 P.M. Book Exhibits

9:00–10:30 A.M. **Panel 8: Documenting in Times of Adversity, Survival and Hope**

Moderator: *Daisy V. Domínguez,* City College of New York, CUNY
Rapporteur: *María Angela Leal,* Oliveira Lima Library, Washington, D.C.

Presenters: *María Rita Corticelli,* University of Exeter
Holly Ackerman, Duke University, Durham
"Beyond Search and Retrieval: The Case of the Cuban Rafter Phenomenon: A Unique Sea Exodus"

Molly Molloy, New Mexico State University, Las Cruces
"The Truth that No One Wants to Know: Preserving the Record of Unprecedented Violence in Ciudad Juárez and the Border Region, 2008–Present"

Lynn Shirey, Harvard University, Cambridge
"Chilean Protest Murals at Harvard"

9:00–10:30 A.M. **Panel 9: Historias y Contenidos en Revistas Latinoamericanas y Españolas**

Moderator: *Philip S. MacLeod,* Emory University, Atlanta
Rapporteur: *Víctor J. Cid Carmona,* Colegio de México, México, DF

Presenters: *Luis Rodríguez Yunta,* CSIC-CCHS, Madrid
"Contenidos latinoamericanos en revistas españolas: dificultades para determinar la colección de publicaciones de Estudios Latinoamericanos"

Marisol Ramos, University of Connecticut, Storrs
Michael J. Bennett, University of Connecticut, Storrs
"Mujeres, Damas y Señoritas: El Mundo de las Revistas Femeninas Españolas del Siglo XIX al Alcance de la Mano: The Women's Magazine Digital Collection at the Thomas J. Dodd Research Center"

Claudia Escobar Vallarta, Colegio de México, México, DF
" 'El Libro y el Pueblo': su contribución al cimiento de la escuela bibliotecológica mexicana (1922–1935)"

9:00–10:30 A.M. **Panel 10: Bridging Physical, Virtual and Hybrid Spaces in Libraries**

Moderator: *Orchid Mazurkiewicz,* Hispanic American Periodicals Index, University of California, Los Angeles
Rapporteur: *Norma Palomino,* Inter-American Development Bank, Washington, D.C.

Presenters: *Angela Carreño,* New York University, New York
"New York University's Experience with the Cloud Library Research Project"

Sarah Buck Kachaluba, Florida State University, Tallahassee
"Approaches to Freeing up Space and Funds in Tight Physical and Fiscal Library Environments: Two Case Studies from FSU Libraries"

Alison Hicks, University of Colorado, Boulder
"Analysing La Cuña: Future Directions for a Digital SALALM"

Pamela Graham, Columbia University, New York
"Radical Collaboration for Extreme Futures: Reflections on 2CUL and Beyond"

9:00–10:30 A.M.   **Panel 11: Rebuilding Haiti's and Chile's Libraries**

Moderator: *Gayle Williams,* Digital Library of the Caribbean, Florida International
                   University, Miami
Rapporteur: *Joseph Holub,* University of Pennsylvania, Philadelphia
Presenters: *Brooke Wooldridge,* Digital Library of the Caribbean, Florida
                   International University, Miami
                   "Saving Haitian Cultural Patrimony after the Earthquake"

                   Michael Dowling, International Relations Office, American Library
                   Association, Chicago
                   "ALA Efforts in Haiti and Chile: Fundraising and Partnering to Rebuild"

11:00 A.M.–12:30 P.M.   **Panel 12: Roundtable on Collaborative Collection Development
                         Part 1: A Survey of Collaborative Collecting Models**

Moderator: *Lynn Shirey,* Harvard University, Cambridge
Rapporteur: *Teresa Miguel,* Yale Law School, New Haven
Presenters: Introduction by *Lynn Shirey,* Harvard University, Cambridge
                   "Collaborative Collection Development for Latin American Studies:
                   A Historical Overview"

                   Discussants: *Teresa Chapa* (University of North Carolina,
                   Chapel Hill); *Eudora Loh* (University of California, Los Angeles);
                   Miguel A. Valladares (Dartmouth College, Hanover)
                   "Current Models of Collaborative Collection Development at SALALM
                   Libraries"

11:00 A.M.–12:30 P.M.   **Panel 13: Caribbean Treasures: Collections and Research Strategies**

Moderator: *Darlene Hull,* Libros de Barlovento, San Juan
Rapporteur: *Tracy North,* Library of Congress, Washington, D.C.
Presenters: *Elmelinda Lara,* University of the West Indies, St. Augustine
                   Kathleen Helenese-Paul, University of the West Indies, St. Augustine
                   "Hidden Treasures Come to Light at the University of the West Indies
                   St. Augustine Campus"

                   Georgette M. Dorn, Library of Congress, Washington, D.C.
                   "Research Strategies and Collections Development: The LC Cuban
                   Collections"

                   Sarah Aponte, Dominican Studies Institute, City College, New York
                   "The Presence of Dominican Studies in the United States: A Unique
                   Library Collection"

11:00 A.M.–12:30 P.M.   **Panel 14: Trends in Technical and Information Services:
                         International Perspectives**

Moderator: *Héctor Morey,* Library of Congress, Washington, D.C.
Rapporteur: *Ellen Jaramillo,* Yale University, New Haven
Presenters: *Tony Harvell,* University of California, San Diego
                   "Future Trends in Acquisitions and Cataloging of Latin American
                   Materials"

                   Sergio Rodríguez Quezada, Biblioteca de Santiago, Chile
                   "Políticas de adquisición bibliográficas en la República de Chile"

                   Geoff West, British Library, London
                   "Tendering for European (Spanish and Portuguese) Monographs:
                   Critical Issues"

Micaela Chávez Villa, Colegio de México, México, DF
Víctor J. Cid Carmona, Colegio de México, México, DF
"La contribución del CLADES de la CEPAL al desarrollo de los sistemas de información en América Latina"

11:00 A.M.–12:30 P.M. **Panel 15: What Is New with Latin American and Spanish E-Journal Content?**

Moderator: Peter Stern, University of Massachusetts, Amherst
Rapporteur: Marne Grinolds, Ohio University, Athens

Presenters: Iría Alvarez, Revista de Libros
"Los lectores de revistas culturales en el entorno digital"

Patricia Martínez, Asociación de Editores de Revistas Culturales de España (ARCE), Madrid
"Pensando en digital: retos y oportunidades: Revistas Culturales de España (ARCE)"

Anne Ray, JSTOR, New York
"JSTOR and Latin American Content"

Elizabeth Brown, Project MUSE, Baltimore
"Project MUSE and Latin American Content"

12:30–2:00 P.M. Lunch

2:00–3:45 P.M. **Panel 16: Roundtable on Collaborative Collection Development Part 2: How to Move Forward**

Moderator: Dan Hazen, Harvard University, Cambridge
Rapporteur: Mark L. Grover, Brigham Young University, Provo

Presenters: Denise Hibay, New York Public Library
"Tools for Collection Analysis"

David Magier, Princeton University
"Emerging Trends and Institutional Frameworks for Collaboration: Borrow Direct and Other Partnerships"

Miguel A. Valladares, Dartmouth College, Hanover
"Mapping New Collecting Collaborations for Latin American Studies"

2:00–3:45 P.M. **Panel 17: Beyond Institutional Borders: Archivists Document Underrepresented Communities**

Moderator: Silvia Mejía, Massachusetts Institute of Technology, Cambridge
Rapporteur: Brenda Salem, University of Pittsburgh

Presenters: Yesenia López, Puerto Rican Community Archives, Newark Public Library
"Organizing Our Communities' Records: Connecting a Community to Its History"

Tomaro I. Taylor, University of South Florida, Tampa
"Web 2.0 and Underrepresented Communities"

Joan D. Krizack, Northeastern University, Boston
"Preserving the History of Boston's Diversity: Northeastern University's Project to Document the African American, Chinese, Latino, and GLBT Communities of Boston"

Pedro Juan Hernández, Centro de Estudios Puertorriqueños, Hunter College, New York
"Becoming Visible: A Profile of the Archives of the Puerto Rican Diaspora at the Centro de Estudios Puertorriqueños"

2:00–3:45 P.M.	**Panel 18: Literature, Culture, Commemorations**
Moderator:	*Georgette M. Dorn,* Library of Congress, Washington, D.C.
Rapporteur:	*Paul Losch,* University of Florida, Gainesville
Presenters:	*Beatriz Colombi,* Universidad de Buenos Aires
	"Pasado y presente de los estudios literarios latinoamericanos en la Argentina"
	Luis M. Villar, Seattle
	"The Sor Juana Ines de la Cruz Online Bibliography"
	Sarah Buck Kachaluba, Florida State University, Tallahassee
	"An Introduction to Eduardo Urzaíz's 'Eugenia' "
	Barbara Tenenbaum, Library of Congress, Washington, D.C.
	"Mexico, Washington, and 2010"
4:00–5:30 P.M.	Committee Meeting
	Library/Bookdealer/Publisher Relations
7:00–10:00 P.M.	Libreros' Reception
	Brown University Faculty Club

Tuesday, July 27, 2010

8:30 A.M.–2:30 P.M.	Book Exhibits
9:00–10:30 A.M.	**Panel 19: Collection Development Strategies for Haitian Studies**
Moderator:	*Dominique Coulombe,* Brown University, Providence
Rapporteur:	*Peter S. Bushnell,* University of Florida, Gainesville
Presenters:	*Alfonso Vijil,* Libros Latinos, San Francisco
	"The Haitian Booktrade 1980–2010 Observations of a U.S. Bookdealer"
	Richard F. Phillips, University of Florida, Gainesville
	"Playing Scrabble in Haitian Creole: Study and Research of Haiti and the Haitian Language at the University of Florida"
	Edward L. Widmer, John Carter Brown Library, Providence
	Leslie Tobias Olsen, John Carter Brown Library, Providence
	"Building a Digital Haitian Library"
9:00–10:30 A.M.	**Panel 20: Social Networks and Archival Acquisitions: Then and Now**
Moderator:	*Sarah Aponte,* Dominican Studies Institute, City College, New York
Rapporteur:	*John Wright,* Brigham Young University, Provo
Presenters:	*Claire-Lise Bénaud,* University of New Mexico, Albuquerque
	"Archive It Old School: Solo Collecting, Networking, and eBay"
	Suzanne M. Schadl, University of New Mexico, Albuquerque
	"Archive It, the Aughties: E-born Special Collections"
	Kevin J. Comerford, University of New Mexico, Albuquerque
	"Archive-It™: A New Acquisition Model for a New Century"
9:00–10:30 A.M.	**Panel 21: Demonstration of e-resources from Spain and Portugal**
Moderator:	*Patricia Figueroa,* Brown University, Providence
Rapporteur:	*Sarah Buck Kachaluba,* Florida State University, Tallahassee
Presenters:	*Patricia Figueroa,* Brown University, Providence
	"Hispana, Biblioteca Digital Hispánica (BDH), Hemeroteca Digital, Biblioteca Virtual de Prensa Histórica, Biblioteca Nacional Digital, PORBASE, Bibliografia Nacional Portuguesa em linha and Patrimonia, Livro Antigo"

Luis Rodríguez Yunta, CSIC, Madrid
Teresa Abejón, CSIC, Madrid
"ISOC—Ciencias Sociales y Humanidades"

Paula Covington, Vanderbilt University, Nashville
"PARES, El Portal de Archivos Españoles and Bibliografía de la
Literatura Española desde 1980"

Miguel Valladares, Dartmouth College, Hanover
"Dialnet, ARCA and Traces"

11:00 A.M.–12:30 P.M.	**Panel 22: Judging by the Cover: Special Collections and Formats**
Moderator:	*Peter S. Bushnell,* University of Florida, Gainesville
Rapporteur:	*Michael R. Scott,* University of North Carolina, Chapel Hill
Presenters:	*Michael T. Hamerly,* John Carter Brown Library, Providence "Andean Language Materials of the Colonial Period at the John Carter Brown Library"
	C. Denise Stuempfle, Indiana University, Bloomington "From Trash to Treasure: Incorporating the Voices of the Marginalized into the Collection of Indiana University Libraries"
	Alyson Williams, University of Wisconsin, Madison *Paloma Celis Carbajal,* University of Wisconsin, Madison "Literatura de Cordel and Holdings at U.S. Libraries"
11:00 A.M.–12:30 P.M.	**Panel 23: Research Resources and Strategies across Disciplines**
Moderator:	*Marne Grinolds,* Ohio University, Athens
Rapporteur:	*Suzanne Schadl,* University of New Mexico, Albuquerque
Presenters:	*David S. Nolen,* Mississippi State University "Secondary Sources in Spanish and Latin American Literary Studies: Language and Place of Publication"
	Teresa Miguel, Yale Law School, New Haven "Researching the Law in Latin America"
	Ruby Gutiérrez, Hispanic American Periodicals Index, Los Angeles *Sócrates Silva,* Hispanic American Periodicals Index, Los Angeles "Searching for the Right Word: The HAPI Thesaurus"
	Ketty Rodríguez, Universidad de Puerto Rico, Río Piedras "Peer-Reviewed Latin American Journals on Business and Management"
11:00 A.M.–12:30 P.M.	**Panel 24: Ebooks: Contents, Possibilities and Challenges**
Moderator:	*Adán Griego,* Stanford University
Rapporteur:	*Geoff West,* British Library, London
Presenters:	*Miguel A. Valladares,* Dartmouth College, Hanover "Spanish Electronic Books and Libraries: They're Already Here!"
	Lluis Claret, DIGITALIA, New York "El Libro electrónico en español: presente y futuro para bibliotecas"
	Felipe Varela, Ebrary/c-libro.com "La Socialización del conocimiento"
12:30–1:30 P.M.	Lunch
1:30–2:30 P.M.	Town Hall Meeting and Announcement of New Officers
2:30–3:30 P.M.	Business Meeting and Closing Session
3:30–5:00 P.M.	Executive Board Meeting #2